THE UNIVERSE IS CALLING

Other Books by Eric Butterworth

The Universe Is Calling

Opening to the Divine
Through Prayer

Eric Butterworth

HarperSanFrancisco

A Division of HarperCollins*Publishers*

Harper San Francisco and the author, in association with the Rainforest Action Network, will facilitate the planting of two trees for every one tree used in the manufacture of this book.

THE UNIVERSE IS CALLING: *Opening to the Divine Through Prayer.* Copyright © 1993 by Eric Butterworth. All rights reserved. Printed in the United States of America. No part of this book may be used or reproduced in any manner whatsoever without written permission except in the case of brief quotations embodied in critical articles and reviews. For information address HarperCollins Publishers, 10 East 53rd Street, New York, NY 10022.

FIRST EDITION

Library of Congress Cataloging-in-Publication Data
Butterworth, Eric.
    The universe is calling : opening to the divine through prayer /
Eric Butterworth.—1st ed.
        p.   cm.
    Includes bibliographical references.
    ISBN 0–06–250998–5 (alk. paper).—ISBN 0–06–250094–5 (pbk.:
alk. paper)
    1. Prayer.   2. Prayer—Christianity.   I. Title.
BL560.B83   1993
291.4′3—dc20   91–59028
                                                                          CIP

93 94 95 96 97 RRD (H) 10 9 8 7 6 5 4 3 2 1

This edition is printed on acid-free paper that meets the American National Standards Institute Z39.48 Standard.

To the universe that is persistently calling . . .
To those on the path who faithfully listen . . .
To Olga, who listens better than anyone I know
and whose great loving support and
patience have given me the time and
inspiration for my listening . . .
and its result:
The Universe Is Calling.

Contents

The Universe Is Calling

Introduction

Through the ages of the unfolding of human creatures on planet Earth, there have been thousands of books and treatises on the subject of prayer. Do we really need another one? Some people might say that the great need of humans is to get back to really praying, not just theorizing about prayer. But what is it to really pray?

People may talk of "saying their prayers." They are speaking words that have been given to them, but in which there is little spontaneity or feeling. We teach our children to say their prayers before they go to bed, and they use words given to them, such as "Now I lay me down to sleep." I am not questioning the process. It is a good discipline, and it may have a positive influence on the child. But it can be terribly misleading. Unless children have the right idea of their relationship with God, they will grow up with a God-up-there attitude, and later in life they will still be "saying their prayers," without the slightest idea of what prayer is or how they should be praying. So there is a great need to unlearn errors. Jesus made it clear to his troubled disciples that though they were praying, they were praying "amiss."

The greatest problem in teaching prayer is the confused attitude toward God that prevails through the world of religion. Michelangelo's classic figure of a muscular God reaching down from the skies, touching the finger of the outstretched hand of a human creature, is a good example of how great works of art have often made for bad theology. It is probably true that most of us have felt the conditioning influence of this dualistic, sexist perception, giving rise to a prayer practice of reaching out and up to the big man of the skies, begging for help and pleading for mercy.

Advice that is so common as to become almost a cliché is "Pray about it!" Slogans such as "Prayer changes things" and "The family that prays together, stays together" stress the importance of prayer, but they are built on the assumption that we know what prayer is. We need to ask such questions as: What do we mean by prayer? How should we pray? When there are so many different religions, each with its own techniques and beliefs, how do we know which is the right approach? How do we know, for instance, that our prayer is heard over the din of millions of praying people all over the world? Or, as Frederick the Great said, "God is always with the strongest battalions."

Are there not underlying principles by which prayer operates? Is it conceivable that prayer could be a science? And if we study the science and come to understand the principles involved, would we not then be able to pray consistently and effectively? It is our thesis that there is such a science . . . and this is what this book is all about.

In embarking on a study of prayer, its meaning and its practice, it is important to understand that we are dealing with a natural function of life, and not with something that is superimposed on our life, something unnatural like raising palm trees in Greenland, where palm trees were never intended to grow. You could not possibly grow palm trees in Greenland unless you used some artificial means. The culture of prayer would be just as strained a procedure were it not true that the tendency toward prayer is indigenous to every person. The human creature is a "praying animal." Some form of prayer comes naturally to all: to an African throwing a stone on the votive pile along the road, a Buddhist using a prayer wheel, a Tibetan tying a prayer flag to a tree, an Indian fakir living on a bed of spikes, or an American farmer nailing a horseshoe over the barn door for good luck.

Recently, the Congress of the United States has been grappling with the question of prayer in schools. In its heated debate, Congress has actually attempted to agree on the meaning and the process of prayer, something not even religious leaders have been able to agree on through ages of theological debate. If an agreement could be reached to have children open their school day with a classroom prayer, and if an inoffensive prayer, acceptable to all religions, could be hammered out, what would be accomplished? Is prayer then simply a verbal formula? A "bargaining chip" with God? And who and where is God?

Impertinent, even sacrilegious, questions, perhaps, but if we are to have any success at all in the practice of prayer, we need to know the field in which we are trying to work. Because tradition has conditioned us to perceive God as up there among billowy clouds, as suggested by Michelangelo's classic painting on the ceiling of the Sistine Chapel, prayer for most persons is reaching out and up, pleading, supplicating, and bargaining.

With this introduction to the subject, let's launch into a study of the science of prayer. We may ask as many questions as we give answers—probably more. We will not presume to be the authority. It is our goal, very simply, to bring light to a religious experience that, for many, has been a groping in the darkness.

It might make your experience with this book easier if we explain a few words that we will be using. Note, we didn't say define. For we agree with the oriental adage, "To define a thing is to limit it." We refer occasionally to "The New Insight in Truth." This is to make clear that *The Universe Is Calling* is a new perception of Truth, a new look at metaphysics, and a new penetrating vision of new thought. We owe no allegiance to the dogma of any organized movement or school. Though the language and many of the metaphors we use are Christian, we are referring to the religion of Jesus, not the religion about Jesus.

A word that crops up frequently in all metaphysical studies is *consciousness*. I call it a "one word religion." It simply means awareness. Your awareness has everything to do with what you are experiencing physically, financially, socially, and even environmentally. By the cumulative, distilled essence of your mentality at any given moment, you draw to yourself all that manifests in your life. And nothing that happens to you or in you is totally unrelated to your consciousness. You are always at least a part of the cause of both good and bad events. But the bright side of this is that you can be healed, you can be successful, you can overcome problems by changing your consciousness.

In this study of prayer we will refer often to meditation. This word may conjure up a scantily clad guru sitting cross-legged on a chaise longue with a demeanor of total bliss. Our practice of meditation will be somewhat less complicated. We will emphasize the need to get ourselves focused in mind, resting in the divine flow that rushes and streams into us from the supportive universe all around. Meditation is the central feature in prayer. It turns the thought in prayer away from trying to reach out and up to God in the attempt to secure his aid. It is reflecting in silence on the source of all mind, all life, all substance dynamically present within us as a potential that can be realized.

The word "affirmation" will be referred to as a vital technique in the practice of prayer. In this new insight, prayer is not something you say or do to God. It is something you consciously let God do to and through you. We will explore the idea that you need not ask God for help. You begin with a consciousness of God and then project it by means of powerful spoken words. However, affirmations are not magic formulas that you build a repertoire of, calling the appropriate statement forth to deal with changing situations. An affirmation is not something you repeat over and over to make something happen. It is accepting the truth of the omnipresence and the everpresence of the good you desire, laying claim to it by a word of truth that says "yes" to its outformation in your life.

You will be confronted repeatedly by two phrases out of the teachings of Jesus. The repetition is by design, for we want the ideals to be emblazoned on your consciousness. For this is how Jesus dealt with the idea that "the universe is calling." Here are the phrases:

"Your Father knows what you need before you ask him" (Matt. 6:8).

"It is your Father's good pleasure to give you the Kingdom" (Luke 12:32).

These are from the teachings of Jesus, and their powerful implications have been overlooked completely in the teachings about Jesus.

The Universe Is Calling may lead you into unfamiliar trails in your quest. Go forward in the spirit of adventure. You have nothing to lose but illness, and you stand to gain a new experience of allness.

Prologue

Come with me to my favorite retreat of the mind. Sit with me in a lovely mountain meadow in a field of golden poppies. And reflect with me on a great thought:

As I snap my fingers, imagine that the earth disappears from beneath us, and we are in space, with the moon and the sun looming large before us. I snap my fingers again, and the moon disappears, and again, and the sun disappears. Now we are deep into "outer space," in a great vault of the universe. We are within a canopy of stars around us on all sides, and they appear to be sending their shafts of light specifically to us, like supporting hands of the universe.

Rest for a while in this image, and feel the universe rushing, streaming, and pouring into you from all sides while you sit quietly. Now you may be wondering, "Is this praying?" Certainly not as the world prays. For you are the center of the universe, or of God. (Is there a difference?) God is a presence who is totally present. So there is nowhere to bow down and worship him, even within yourself. Can you sense the awakening to a new insight into God and yourself? Not someone to pray to, but the "focus of an infinite idea" being projected into visibility as you, that you pray from.

The universe is calling. It is the call of Prometheus, a restless urge that keeps you forever reaching for the highest, and is incapable of settling for anything less. It is an inner voice that whispers, "This is not good enough. Life must be more than this. There must be a better way to live."

The call of the universe is like the pull of the sun on the sunflower, which causes the blossoms to open up and face the sun continuously as it crosses the sky. It is the pull of life upward and outward on all growing things. It is the healing activity in which life is always biased on the side of health. "Many are called, but few are chosen," said Jesus (Matt. 22:14). This is not suggesting discrimination. It is the universe calling, and it is a continuum, innate in all persons. It is the call to come up higher, to take charge of your life, to release your imprisoned splendor. The universe is calling, but sadly, few persons respond with a commitment to make progressive changes in their lives.

The call of the universe is the key to prayer, though it is not prayer as we have been conditioned to perceive it. Your prayer is not for God to listen to. True prayer is words that God may utter through you . . . that you voice, or feel in the silence. You may recall that Jesus said, "The word which you hear is not mine but the Father's who sent me" (John 14:24).

. . . We are brought back from the imaging experience by the loud "Bong! Bong! Bong!" of the bells in the cathedral over on the hill . . . which suggests a brilliant metaphor: The weather vane on the steeple is pointing north. But it does not make the north wind blow. It simply registers the direction of the wind. And when we pray, we do not cause God to spring into action. Rather, in our praying, we are hearing the call of the universe and responding to it. Perhaps it is a startling insight—but think about it. Try it.

The universe is calling . . . are you listening?

PART ONE

PITFALLS OF PRAYER

CHAPTER 1

A Short History of Prayer

The poet sings, "Hope springs eternal in the human breast."[1] The reason is that every normal person has wishes and dreams of better things. Within every person there is an intuitive sense of the transcendent, an inner knowledge that there is more to life than one is experiencing, and a yearning to unfold more of that more. No matter how realistic or humanistic we may be, we still look up. We have aspirations and dream "impossible dreams" that here and there have become possible. It is this sense of the transcendent that has lit the fires on every altar, built every temple and shrine, made every creed articulate, and supported every prayer through all history. It is the Universe calling to human creatures, relentlessly urging them to "come up higher."

It is widely but erroneously believed that religion began with a complete conscious relationship with God, and then in the ages that followed, through weakness and sin, and through the supposed "fall of man," we lost sight of that first splendid vision. This is a concept that prevails through much of our traditional religion. And it is one of the first religious ideas that the thinking person begins to question, even resist, finding it difficult to accept a theology that is essentially preoccupied with looking backward.

Most religions look back to a golden age of their spiritual giants, a time when "God walked the earth." The Jewish tradition looks back to the days of Abraham, Isaac, Jacob, and Moses. Christianity looks backward to the days of Jesus, and to the adventures and writings of Paul. Thus, the traditionalists of religion invariably deal with worship in retrospect.

Actually, the assembled records of archaeology and anthropology indicate a progressive evolution of culture and consciousness throughout all history, including biblical history. We have nothing to lead us to believe that this evolutionary flow suddenly stopped along the way. When we consider the primitive creatures in their worship of sticks and stones, we are not seeing evidence of religion in decay. We are seeing an early level of consciousness from which later and more elevated forms evolved.

Primitive creatures were fire-worshipers and sun-worshipers. They were terribly insecure creatures, stricken with mortal fear of all the elements, who often created their own gods. But it would be incorrect to say that they did not pray. A kind of praying impulse was a part of the fiber of their being—a dim perception of their relationship with the universe. However dim or vague, there was that feeling that Longfellow articulates:

14

That even in savage bosoms,
There are longings, yearnings, strivings
For the good they comprehend not,
That the feeble hands and helpless,
Groping blindly in the darkness,
Touch God's right hand in that darkness
And are lifted up and strengthened.[2]

One of the grave mistakes that we make in our study of primitive cultures of the far-distant past, and even now in studying undeveloped parts of the world, is to refer to the people as *pagans*. In the study of religion, the concept of *paganism* is an unfortunate one. Let's look at this word, understand it, and then make a commitment to eliminate it from our vocabulary. From our Christian or Jewish background, we have used the word *pagan* to mean *nonbeliever*, coming from a feeling that "my God" is the "only God," and anyone who believes in any other "god" is stupid—thus a pagan.

The word *pagan* comes from the same root as *village*, and *peasant*. The word was originally used by a sophisticated (?) city dweller in describing a person from a rural area (a "hick from the sticks"). Even before this, it was used in general reference to people who came from the country—the hill areas (*hillbillies*). In that period, Christianity was sweeping through the world in the predominantly urban areas, even as today liberalism has its greatest support in urban centers, and is slow to take hold in rural farm and ranch areas. So it was common in the early days of the spread of Christianity to refer to those people who came from the hinterlands, and who were still holding to pre-Christian or non-Christian attitudes and practices, as *pagans*. At best this was unkind, and at worst it was a dangerous root of prejudice and an ethnic slur. Much of this cultural putdown originated with the Christian missionaries who labeled as *pagans* people in the cultures of Africa, China, India, and the native Indians in America.

From the earliest of times, people have had a need to symbolize their sense of the transcendent. They have had an instinctive reverence for any power or powers that they believed might help or harm them. So when a bolt of lightning struck and killed a brother, they were possessed by a sudden fear of lightning, which in their primitive mind was interpreted as reverence. The lightning became a god. Soon the primitive creatures built an altar to the new god, on which they made sacrifices of appeasement to prevent the lightning from doing them further harm.

In early times, and even, surprisingly, in relatively sophisticated cultures, the sacrifice was in the form of human flesh. Later, the practice evolved into a mere symbolic gesture. We may have a more realistic understanding of the Bible if we note that the practice of human sacrifice as a form of the worship of Yahweh was still a strong memory as the Bible narrative burst upon the evolutionary scene. A glaring example is that instance where Abraham took his son, Isaac, up on a mountain, with the intent of sacrificing his life to Yahweh. That he was dissuaded at the last moment from this act of human sacrifice should not blind us to the fact of its possibility in Abraham's culture at that time.

Burnt offerings and animal flesh were a central part of Temple worship all through the Old Testament. With lines of squealing lambs being led to slaughter, smoke burning the eyes, and obnoxious odors emanating from the ceremonies of worship, the "house of God" was not a very pleasant place to go for contemplation. Shocking as it may be to consider, the richly adorned altar of the modern church is the carryover of the veritable butcher block on which life was once slaughtered. Such is the evolution of a ritual.

The Hebrew prophets cried out for reform. If you are interested, you might read Isaiah 1:11–17. However, the slaughter of animals on the altar continued almost up to the time of Jesus. We can sense this in the view (articulated in prayer and song) that Jesus was the "lamb of God" who was sacrificed at the altar of the Lord to take away the sins of mankind. It is the basis of that most hideous of Christian concepts, the "vicarious atonement." It was and is an interesting commentary on the God-concepts that did (and do) prevail.

We must keep in mind that "the gods," and later, under Moses, the "one God," evolved from human imagination. God was the symbol of the unknown, of an intuitive belief in a universe of law and order. And the Old Testament of the Bible is the chronicle of a slow evolution from the primitive anthropomorphic view of deity all the way up to Jesus' concept of a loving and tender presence that is ever-present. Along the way, the God that was portrayed was wrathful and jealous and vindictive, giving life and taking it away with impunity, at times viciously destroying entire cities. For a liberal education in realism, read 1 Samuel 15:3.

Out of this concept of God evolved the doctrine of "God's will." God brings troubles and even death to us, supposedly for some inscrutable reason he has. Thus, if only we can get God's ear and prove our penitence through offerings and sacrifices, our fervent plea may be heard and our prayers answered. At least this is what we have been taught. Elaborate prayer doctrines have been built on this structure of confusion of God and the nature of the universe. The healing idea in Protestantism is usually dealt with under the label of "intercessory prayer." It implies that one must plead with God to attain healing, implying that he has either willed the condition or at least acquiesced in it. So, through pleading and bargaining, we hope that God may have second thoughts, saying, "Well, I guess John is sincere in his penitence, and he does seem worthy. I will take a chance on him. I will heal him."

We may wonder, too, how all our complicated rituals came about. The church all but insists that these are set down by God. If we look to earlier times, we see that prayer for the primitive creatures was unstudied and spontaneous. Often it was a simple outcry of the human heart seeking help and protection, reaching for something more. We see this colorfully demonstrated in the Native American who went alone to a high hill and, with his head imperiously held high, looked out into the vastness of the heavens with outstretched arms, in a kind of embrace of the whole universe. His prayer was unstudied, spontaneous, wordless—no incantation, no ritual, no repetition of words. In some way he had a subconscious feeling of the wholeness of things. Perhaps he sensed with Gibran that prayer is the expansion of oneself into the living ether.

Prayer and worship became formalized, ritualized, but not as a more effective means of communication with God. It was, rather, because of the trend toward specialization in urban societies. In any tribal organization individuals were assigned special duties, one of which was the role of the medicine man or tribal priest, whose duty it was to keep the evil spirits away. Thus, while the others went off hunting or waging war, the designated person ("the holy man") remained behind to keep the purifying fires and to scatter the magic dust on the ground. With obvious modifications, we can see this system at work under Moses' leadership of the Israelites in the wilderness. The completely disorganized mass of ex-slaves was formed into twelve tribes. One of the tribes, the Levites, was designated as the "Priestly Tribe." Actually, since the government being formed was a theocracy, the Levites became the bureaucracy, with the tithes and offerings to the Temple representing a form of taxation.

We can see this practice of specialization today in the minister or priest or rabbi who is given the responsibility to do the praying. It is something like having a lobbyist in Congress. The clergyman is the lobbyist with God, pleading your case, interceding with the divine will. The clergyman is the prayer specialist, so a lay person who prays at all simply uses the formal prayers, incantations, or even affirmations furnished by the minister. This is seen at its most ludicrous when someone comes to a spiritual counselor for prayer help, outlines the problem, and then, possibly dropping a contribution on the desk, says, "Take care of it for me, will you?"

It is a serious point. Let's think about it. Another person can't breathe for you, nor do the praying for you in the sense that it is something extraneous to you, any more than I, if I were a physical culturist, could exercise your lungs for you. I may help you to understand the breathing process so that you can learn how to breathe more efficiently for yourself. But "you make the difference"—and so it is with prayer. Prayer is an individual experience, a matter of understanding your whole self. In chapter 10 we will deal at length with the process of praying for others, making clear that our prayers may help to create an environment in which the other persons can more easily release their own inner power. But in the end the responsibility for that release is still their own.

People talk of "saying their prayers." The words may be read from a prayer book or recited from memory. A typical source of prayers formulated for contemporary use centuries ago is *The Book of Common Prayer*. And the "Lord's Prayer" may be repeated by rote, in a rapid delivery of words that have, for most people, lost their meaning if not their place in personal devotion. In physics we are told that action and reaction are equal. If prayer is the action, and that action consists of the mere recitation of words or the unfeeling performance of a ritual, then the reaction is also quite likely to be ineffective. Little wonder that many thinking people question the validity of the practice of prayer as a reasonable approach to life's experiences.

Prayer, for most of us, playing out the traditional worship practices that have evolved from tribal rituals of antiquity, may be something we hurl at God. It may be a performance put on for eyes and ears other than our own. It is important for every person to make a careful examination of their own personal God-concept. This means honestly and courageously stepping back from the liturgy, even the Mass, of one's church. It doesn't have to mean an act of rebellion against the "faith of our fathers." Rather, it means that we need to discover ourselves as individual expressions of the universe, and to know that there is a kind of personal prayer that is turning within, knowing our oneness with the source, and, through affirmation (not supplication), giving way to the creative process. We can't let our grandfather do our thinking (or praying) for us. You may think that you have a good understanding of God as spirit, and with Emerson you insist upon having a firsthand and immediate experience of God. And yet when you pray, either silently or in public, you may act out your childhood perceptions, talking to God, reaching out and up to God, bargaining, supplicating.

Emerson challenges us to break with the God of tradition, that God may fire us with his presence. It may be startling to you to hear it, but both the Scriptures and the historical church deal with an absence of God, "a worship in retrospect." This may explain the deep feelings of perplexity, even futility, in the praying person. You don't discover God in your worship in the

21

church. You uncover God in yourself, even if by the inspiration of the moving liturgy. But the important thing is, you do not leave God there in the sanctuary. You take him with you, and he will be with you in the street, in your home, in your work, and in every activity of your life. Discover God's presence. God is an allness in which you exist as an eachness. As I say in *Discover the Power Within You,*

> God is not in you in the same sense that a raisin is in a bun. That is not unity. God is in you as the ocean is in a wave. The wave is nothing more nor less than the ocean expressing as a wave.[3]

In his *Divine Milieu,* Teilhard de Chardin says that we come to a place where there is no one to bow down to and worship, not even within ourselves. And as we get a greater perception of our relation to the universe, there is no one to pray to . . . only a universal flow to get into, a spiritual energy to pray from. And the role of prayer is the projection by our words and feelings of this divine flow, this powerful spiritual energy, that goes forth to accomplish that for which it is sent.

The science of prayer is not a technique for getting into God, or for getting God into us. School yourself on this point. It is the awareness of our true self in its largest possible context, and the key to changing things by altering our self-limiting attitudes. What the history of prayer may fail to reveal to us is that there is a secret place at the heart of us where "the Father and I are one." It is this that Jesus had in mind when he said,

". . . enter into thy closet, and when thou hast shut thy door, pray to thy Father which is in secret; and thy Father which seeth in secret shall reward thee openly" (Matt. 6:6, KJV). Prayer is the secret door to cosmic power—not a liturgical rubric bound to ancient tradition, but a consciousness rooted in the here and now.

So prayer is not something we do *to* God, or a ceremony we perform *for* God. It is an experience of our own God-potential. As this book unfolds, we will stress the idea again and again that we do not really pray *to* God, rather we pray *from* a consciousness of God. Prayer is not conditioning God with our needs, but conditioning our lives with the activity of God. Prayer is self-realization, self-expansion. It is getting recentered within, and re-establishing ourselves in the flow of the infinite creative process.

There have been so many powerful realizations of the presence of God and the within-ness of prayer in the writings of poets, saints, and mystics, down through the ages, that one wonders how we could have failed to grasp it—holding tenaciously to the anthropomorphic concept of God sitting "up there" on a billowy cloud, with a long white beard and a big black book.

Significant are the lines of Wordsworth:

> . . . a sense sublime
> Of something far more deeply interfused,
> Whose dwelling is the light of setting suns,

And the round ocean and the living air,
And the blue sky, and in the mind of man:
A motion and a spirit, that impels
All thinking things, all objects of all thought,
And rolls through all things.[4]

CHAPTER 2

The Miracle Trap

Since we are dealing with prayer as a science, it is important to confront the matter of miracles early in the book. For many persons, prayer is confused with the effort to work miracles. But there are no miracles in science. And there are no miracles in God. That may be a shocking statement, to some almost sacrilegious. But before you lay the book aside in protest, hear me out.

Recently I received a brilliantly colored sticker in the mail, intended for a bulletin board or a car bumper: "EXPECT A MIRACLE!" Well-intentioned enthusiasts for the "New Insight in Truth" have printed up thousands of these slogans to encourage faith in things working out in a positive way—a very worthy cause. But however enticing it may be to hope for divine intervention on your behalf, I say, "Don't expect a miracle!" If you center your consciousness on the expectation of miracles, you are playing Russian roulette with universal law, hoping for some cosmic sleight of hand to reach into your life and bring about changes. It is putting the full weight of your consciousness on the side of belief in a universe of caprice.

God doesn't deal in miracles. God is the wholeness of life, substance, and intelligence which is always present. It is not a miracle that is needed, ever, but the discipline of consciousness to let "Thy kingdom come, thy will be done, on earth as it is heaven."

The "pray for a miracle" attitude is often an unwillingness to take charge of one's own life, to take responsibility for one's experience. And when we fail to take responsibility for our experiences, we look for the cause of our problems and needs "out there" in what he did, or what they failed to do; in the weather, the economy, or bad luck. But when we insist that the cause of conditions is outside of us, the change can only come from a change of conditions or fortune out there. In prayer, then, we are looking to God to change things for us. But God can do no more for you than he can do through you.

In some way you have participated in the problem that may be manifesting itself in your life. That is what consciousness is all about. Thus, to effect change, you must participate in the solution by changing your consciousness. Paul said, " . . . be transformed by the renewal of your mind . . . " (Rom. 12:2). He does not say, be transformed by having a miraculous power possess you from outside. No! . . . by the renewal of your mind.

A miracle is defined as a violation of the laws of nature. Of course, this is an absurdity based on a lack of understanding of what we call natural law. Henry Drummond says that science can hear nothing of a "great exception."

There are no laws in nature, there are only laws *of* nature, which are descriptions we have made of our perception of the way the universe functions. Scientists do not "discover" laws of nature, they invent them to describe the facts they find. The "laws" are mere descriptions of what has occurred in the past, and what they have reason to believe will occur in the future. A book on chemistry, botany, or even astronomy, is merely history.

There can be no violation of natural law. For if it is truly law, there can be no exceptions. If there are exceptions, then the so-called law must be revised. If the biblical account of the axe-head floating on the water (2 Kings 6:5-6) is literally true, then there are fundamentals of nature involved of which we are not as yet aware. That is all.

It is precisely because of our tendency to read magic into the stories of the Bible that any practical implications they may have for today has been ignored. We have been profoundly influenced by the artist's attempt to visualize events and to depict Marc Connelly's great figure of God, who says in his *Green Pastures*, "I guess I will rar' back an' pass a miracle."[1] This tendency to read supernatural phenomena into the accounts has often obscured the express instruction about a perfectly natural cause.

The parting of the Red Sea, for example, is quite clearly explained as being caused by "a strong east wind all night"

(Exod. 14:21). The miracle, if such it was, was in the timing. The Israelites crossed at low tide, and the Egyptian forces were swept away by the inrushing return of the waters at high tide. The account clearly says " . . . the sea returned to its wonted flow when the morning appeared . . . and the Lord routed the Egyptians in the midst of the sea" (Exod. 14:27). However, the expect-a-miracle groups have perpetuated the myth of Cecil B. De Mille's God reaching down from on high and damming up walls of water with his great hands.

It is important to note that Jesus clearly says " . . . he who believes in me [in truth], will also do the works that I do; and greater works than these will he do . . . " (John 14:12). While everyone was calling them miracles, he was simply calling his healings his "works." He knew and practiced the healing art because he understood the mental and spiritual laws governing healing. Jesus in his life gave full expression to the Christ principle. This Christ principle is the whole person of each one of us, truly "our hope of glory." When Jesus said, "He who believes in me," he meant anyone who believes in his or her own wholeness. And from this point of wholeness, all things are possible.

Many persons pray for a miracle in a critical situation, when all that is needed is the acceptance of the truth that what they want may be beyond their normal experience, but not beyond the power of the creative process within them. Why should it be a miracle or supernatural phenomenon for any of us to be healed of illness? Isn't that which created us and sustains us capable of making us whole?

It is essentially a matter of semantics, of perceptions and expectations. But to talk of miracles in a given situation is a very subtle form of defeatism. So when I say, "Don't expect a miracle," I am certainly not expressing skepticism of the tremendous power to heal or prosper or adjust, or questioning the full implication of the statement, "All things are possible." For when we deal with changeless spiritual law, we have even greater faith in the wonder-working process. But we don't have to play games.

Of course, when we work with divine law from the highest perspective, the unusual will become commonplace, and wonderful things will begin to occur. But, I say again, don't fall into the "miracle trap," for by so doing you will tend to give up control of your life. Take charge . . . with a willingness to be a part of the solution of your challenges. The working out of your good need not be limited to a "miracle" coming out of the caprice of God. "Greater things shall you do"—even exceeding the miracles conceived by your shaky faith. "All things are possible." All things!

To one who has been obsessed with a personal weakness, hoping to overcome it might seem like reaching for the moon. Now that we have witnessed a moon landing and seen astronauts walking on the surface of the moon, that cliché has lost its validity, hasn't it? It is not even true to say about your weakness, "But this is simply the way I am." The weakness or limiting habit began as an early tendency, as a reaction to life, which in time became a pattern. But if your subconscious mind could learn a pattern of negativity, it can also learn a new positive pattern. No matter how long or how severely you have been in the clutches of alcoholism or some other addiction, no divine intervention or dramatic miracle is required for your healing. You can change. You don't have to be "that way." You can find great help through prayer. But as you come to understand the science of prayer, you will realize that it is not an act of entreaty to God. It is turning the focus of your consciousness away from the problem to your center of being in God, and giving way to the creative flow which will stream forth therapeutically from within your innermost self.

So . . . again, don't fall into the trap of expecting miracles to remove your addictions or to solve your problems. Don't reduce your practice of truth to playing games with divine law. If you really believe you are entitled to the fullness of the Kingdom, the results may appear miraculous, for wonderful things can and will be done. However, this is the natural fulfillment of divine law. The healing you long for, the overcoming you desire, the prosperity and success you have been spiritually working for, do not call for miracles, but for the disciplined application of divine law and the steady effort to know God.

The great ideal of spiritual seeking is to be in tune with the infinite. To traffic in such thoughts as "Only a miracle can save him" and "It is impossible, but I expect a miracle" is to be in tune with the *indefinite*. Prayer is a science, and there are no miracles in science. There are no miracles in an orderly universe. All things are possible.

Henry David Thoreau says it all in these lines from his essay, "Walden":

If one advances confidently in the direction of his dreams, and endeavors to live the life which he has imagined, he will meet with a success unexpected in common hours. He will put some things behind, will pass an invisible boundary; new, universal, and more liberal laws will begin to establish themselves around and within him; or the old laws be expanded, and interpreted in his favor in a more liberal sense, and he will live with the license of a higher order of beings.[2]

CHAPTER 3

What about Karma?

The Greek philosopher Zeno held that the most important aspect of the learning process is to unlearn our errors. In the study of prayer we must "unlearn" the many errors that color our thinking about the prayer process. Like Jesus' disciples of old, most persons today are puzzled as to why, when they pray about something, nothing happens. Jesus answered their puzzlement by saying, "You ask and receive not because you ask amiss" (James 4:3, ASV).

Since the turn of the twentieth century there has been a vast and growing interest among Americans in the religions of the East. This phenomenon is probably due to the failure of Western religions to fulfill the needs of their followers, in terms of their spiritual quest. Much of the interest has been dictated by the passing fancy, the fad of the day, the "in" thing. Thus a steady parade of "gurus," "perfect masters," and "instruments of God" has taken the country by storm.

By this influence there has been an infusion of many ideas of Hindu origin into the language of the Western truth-seeker . . . ideas such as *meditation, self-realization, mantra,* and a great emphasis on *karma.* The latter must be addressed and understood before we can become proficient in the science of prayer. Many persons have bought into the idea of karma wholesale, unaware of its implicit negatives, or the vast and irreconcilable differences between karma and "the law of causation" as Jesus taught it, with its moderating concept of grace and love.

The word *karma* is used widely through much of the literature in the "New Thought" field. Thus, most students have unthinkingly made it a part of their spiritual vocabulary. I think that we need to take a good, long look at the word, and possibly rethink the advisability of identifying with it in our personal practice of the truth. For some this may be difficult, and you may be reluctant to let go of a concept that has colored your whole awareness of truth. To you I say, consider this chapter with the same open mind that has characterized your journey in consciousness out of the bondage of orthodoxy into the new freedom in truth.

There are three basic laws of Hinduism, which are at the root of its various branches:

- The law of identification
- The law of karma
- The law of reincarnation

Admittedly, this is an oversimplification for the purposes of this basic comparison.

The law of identification holds that each person is an eternal being, a soul or *atman*, who is on the pathway of unfoldment toward the ultimate merging into the soul of God. Every practice of the various religions of the East is directed toward realization of oneness with God.

The law of karma, more than anything else, explains the Hindu outlook on life. The word is loosely translated as *destiny* or *fate*. You are what you are, in respect to your fortune and your place in life, because of your karma. Karma fixes the consequences of your acts. All mistakes, failures, and sins must be atoned for in some way at some time. They become a karmic debt that must ultimately, from lifetime to lifetime, be paid. In the Eastern belief, karma explains everything in one's world: suffering, blessing, sorrow, joy, pauper and prince, the pitifully sick and the radiantly healthy. Nothing one does is ever lost, nothing is unaccounted for, nothing is forgotten, discarded, or irrelevant.

The law of reincarnation is, to the Hindu, a cosmic plan whereby the individual is in a continuous succession of births and rebirths through which it is possible to attain perfection in God. The soul, at death, merely seeks out another opportunity to live a life, to be born again to another parent.

You might be thinking, in considering these three laws of Hinduism, "It's just like truth! It is precisely what I believe!" Certainly it does indicate the similarities of the teachings of East and West. Religion is but a way of seeing truth. In the beginning, every religion was a sincere attempt to communicate a vision of truth to the world. It came as a wave washing at the shore of civilization. But as the wave has continued to break on the shore, it has brought the muddied backwash of form and ritual. If we push past the outward forms to the underlying truths, we find great similarities.

On the surface, the concept of karma would appear to be the equivalent of the Western concept of "the law of compensation" of Jesus—"Whatever a man sows, that he will also reap" (Gal. 6:7). The law of karma is simply a statement of a fundamental law of the universe. The universe is one of absolute integrity . . . so it is that one receives what one earns. One cannot receive less than one earns, nor can one receive more. Either would be an infraction of the law of perfect balance.

It is probably true that everyone, at times, may feel sorry for themselves, believing that they are not receiving their just dues. They may cry out that something has been kept from them, that another person has taken their place, or that money or position has been unjustly snatched from them. But there is an inexorable law involved. And so . . . we always set the tone, the standard, of our tomorrows, in the way we deal with the world today. This is a fundamental law, the law of sequence and consequence, or, if you will, the law of consciousness, or karma to the Hindu.

When we understand the way mind works, we realize that to focus our thought on negatives, we use the creative power of thought in a negative way; we literally generate pools of negative energy that will have to be experienced in our lives. Most persons are completely unaware how very negative the tenor of their thoughts is, and how they are constantly laying traps for themselves, building up sequences in mind which will inexorably manifest themselves as consequences of experience.

You see, the universe and everything in it is whole. Mind and body, consciousness and experience, are completely interrelated. And the law of consciousness, or cause and effect (of karma?), is inexorably involved. Every condition in your present life is the result of your consciousness. Your body, your weight, your health are all the outformation of consciousness. Your relationship or the absence of a happy relationship are the consequences of sequences of thought built up over your life. Your prosperity or lack of success is an exact reflection of the causal forces you have, however unconsciously, set in motion. Some would call this the accumulation of karma. I prefer to call it consciousness.

The intimation of this "great law" (identify it as you will) is that you cannot get something for nothing, you cannot break the law without "paying the piper," and the good you do returns to you in some way with certainty. If everyone understood this law and lived by it, their lives would be transformed. There would be no "hoping" for good fortune, no playing the wheel of chance (lottery, numbers, roulette, horse races, and sporting events). In other words, we would see the folly of trying to bypass the great law . . . that success is not getting there but earning the right to be there.

Of course, in our search for meaning we all can see instances where there seems to be an injustice, where life seems unfair. Some people seem to break the law with impunity and get away with it. Some persons seem lucky or unlucky in everything: card-playing, love-making, and the pursuit of money.

Look around you. Where is the justification for the misery and inequality in the world? How can you justify the millions of starving people . . . brutal wars . . . the victims of terrorist attacks and senseless crimes . . . the hungry and homeless all around us?

We are dealing with consciousness. And hard as it sometimes is to accept, there are no experiences unrelated to consciousness. It is like a bank balance where you have an accumulation of pluses or an overwhelming balance of minuses. And this is what is normally explained as an evidence of karma.

I certainly do not accept the idea that karma explains everything, but in its cause and effect aspect, it is an important window into reality. The person who is involved in some accident or tragedy was in some way motivated to be there at that time.

Of course there are times when it is obvious that we cannot understand life in terms of the brief span beginning with birth and ending with death. Thus, the cosmic bank account must carry over from one life experience to another. This is why the idea of reincarnation seems credible. Personally, I find no sense of meaning in life without it.

But now, having said all this, let us note the great and irreconcilable difference between the classic concept of karma and the truth of the law of compensation. The Eastern concept centers on our past and ultimate destiny. There is little hope or promise of freedom today. Karma becomes a cycle of penalty and retribution that continues on from one incarnation to the next. The person is in effect chained to a relentlessly moving wheel by the accumulated effects of the sins of past lives. Thus each person is a weary treadmill traveler from birth to death, and from death to birth.

The resulting effect on the Hindu is a sense of hopelessness and futility. There is no healing, no way to overcome, no way out. Today's problems are part payment for past sins, and the karmic debt must be paid. Retribution must run its course. Now, we should say here that as with all religious philosophies, there are many variations of belief about karma, so it is dangerous to generalize. I am referring to the classic and basic concept of karma.

As we have said, many students of truth have bought into the concept of karma, and have unwittingly accepted a lot of ideas that are irreconcilable with Jesus' teachings, thinking of karma as God's judgment, something that is going to see that we get punished for our sins. But I do not believe in a God or a karmic law that punishes — not even a cause and effect that punishes. You are punished, not *for* your sins, but *by* them.

The great dynamic of Jesus' teaching is, "You will know the truth, and the truth will make you free" (John 8:32). You see, Jesus did accept the karmic law, but he taught that sequences and consequence, cause and effect, are law for matter and mind only, not for spirit. There is no law of retribution in God. For we are told, "I have loved you with an everlasting love" (Jer. 31:3). We are loved unconditionally. God never stops loving us, but we stop loving ourselves.

No matter what the causes of the karmic debt, the effects can be dissolved by "knowing the truth," by raising our consciousness above the level of sin. A good contemporary illustration would be flying out of the earth's gravitational field into outer space, where weight is nullified.

Many persons, hooked on the idea of karma, think that they are restricted by what they call "my karma." It is a rationalization for a feeling of spiritual impotence, and to think this way is to cloud the issue of prayer with the incurability and impossibility that rise out of a sense that karma must run its course. People are often not aware of this, but it is implied when we make mistaken use of the idea of karma at all.

The dynamic of prayer (often overlooked by Christians) is that when you "enter into thine inner chamber and shut the door" (Matt. 6:6, ASV), you enter the realm of spiritual consciousness where the higher law of spirit overrides or supersedes the lower law of the mental and physical realms. Thus the new insight in truth reveals the way to freedom from karma. Retribution can be transcended, the cycle of karma can be broken. You can be free, all debts dissolved, you can be healed . . . through the Christ indwelling.

Paul says, "For the law was given through Moses; grace and truth came through Jesus Christ" (John 1:17, ASV). Let's look at this thing called grace.

CHAPTER 4

Concerning Grace

Few words in Christian theology are used more or understood less than the word *grace*. Often heard are such phrases as *God's grace* and *the grace of our Lord Jesus Christ*. What does the word mean? How does it work in our lives? In theology the word is surrounded by an air of mystery. Actually it is a very simple explanation of the natural flow of the creative process in the individual.

The word *grace* means favor. Why are you favored as a child of God? Simply because you are the activity of God expressing himself as you. Why is your hand favored as a part of your body? Because it is your body at the point of your hand, designed to enable the body to carry out its objectives. Thus the hand has not only strength, but also feeling and tenderness.

God's will is another confused religious term. As long as we think of God as willfully bombarding our lives with capricious acts of limitation, there is little hope that we can grasp the science of prayer. The will of God for you is the ceaseless longing of the creator to fulfill himself in and as that which he has created. If you miss this point you will think of grace as a kind of favoritism that you solicit through prayer. This will or creative intention is so great that, despite the power of the spoken word, you could say with feeling, "I wish I were dead!" and yet go right on living. God's will for you is so intense, so continuous, that it even filters through your willfully closed mind.

Grace is not a special movement in mind, or a special activity or gift of God. It is simply an explanation of the way mind works. Grace explains the inadequacy of the idea of karma, the endless cycle of cause and effect. It is true that "as you sow so shall you reap." Yet, God's desire to express through you and as you is so great that you never completely reap the harvest of error, and you always reap more good than you sow. A medical researcher says that the body is biased on the side of health. This is the grace factor that is absent in the classic concept of karma.

The missing link in the teachings of the East is that we are not lonely pilgrims on the path, trying to reach something in God. We are dynamic expressions of God on the quest to know and release something in ourselves. We may limit the flow of good, but we can always know the truth and be free.

You are not a helpless creature bobbing about like a cork on the seas of life, at the mercy of the storms of fate and circumstance. You are the very self-livingness of God. When you desire spiritual growth, it is God who has first desired it in you. When you make an extra effort in your work, it is the divine urge in you that is working through you. You are not simply a subject of God, with God making notations of sin and error, or of good, in his big black book. You are the activity of God in expression, beloved with an everlasting love.

Living in a state of grace is an expression often used to imply that the person has earned God's favor. It may be made to appear that by joining a church, or accepting a particular religious cliché, you get something special . . . that it's like knowing someone at City Hall who arranges to "fix" parking tickets.

Living in a state of grace can mean nothing more nor less than living in a disciplined awareness of the divine flow. God's flow is constant. Our experience of it changes with our consciousness.

This does not minimize the universal law of sequence and consequence. In the horizontal experience of life, we are bound to reap as we have sowed, but we have a choice to introduce into consciousness the vertical flow. Thus, on a higher level of consciousness, we are set free. We still pay the price, but on a higher level. It is like turning on a light. Darkness is no longer a factor.

The law of consciousness is inviolable. The high consciousness heals, and the low consciousness weakens. However, something of the infinite is always filtering through and becoming part of your consciousness. Thus, the most sordid or limited thought is modified by God's love in you. Grace is like living in a house with every door and window tightly closed. Invariably, there is enough air leaking in around doors and windows so that your oxygen needs are met.

Grace, as the divine favor, the activity of God's love, is working for you constantly. It is not dependent upon any special faith or prayer on your part. Like the buoyancy of water that will keep you afloat even when you try to force yourself under, grace fulfills divine law by sustaining you in spite of yourself.

You don't have to earn grace. It is not something that comes only to the good. It comes to all alike, because all alike are expressions of God. By the grace of God, a criminal is still loved by God and can still find forgiveness and ultimate rehabilitation through a love that transcends law.

Grace is simply a wonderful facet of the activity of God in you. It is not something you must work for or develop. It simply is. It is an assurance, an explanation of why things are never quite hopeless, and why we never receive the full harvest of the error we sow, and why we always receive a little more good than we earn.

Certainly, we must be willing to accept responsibility for all that is manifest in our lives. But don't get bogged down in the grim and fatalistic acceptance of "working out your karma." Truth can set you free. And when you hear, "He was healed by God's grace," remember that this is no special act of God for one person, but a specialization of the divine "good pleasure" that is in every person.

There is an upward pull of the universe, ever seeking to lift you to the heights of your divine nature. It is as real and as inexorable as the force of gravity. The universe is calling . . . are you listening?

PART TWO

THE PRAYER PROCESS

CHAPTER 5

The Cosmic Counterpart

Through the ages human creatures have used prayer to try to overcome unwanted conditions in their lives. In earlier times there were prayers of sacrifice to placate an angry God. There are prayers of praise in the hope that a vain God might answer because he is pleased by flattery. There are prayers of supplication in which the one praying hopes to coax a miracle from a reticent God. There are prayers of repetition in the hope that, if one asks long enough and strong enough, an apparently preoccupied or inattentive God might finally hear and respond. And there are the prayers of invocation, such as those "delivered" by a clergyman at the opening of a political convention, which begin with "Dear Lord" and end with "Amen" and have a rousing political speech in between.

It never ceases to amaze me how Jesus' teachings about prayer, which are so plain and simple, have been overlooked throughout Christendom. In his preface to what has been called "The Lord's Prayer," which itself is greatly misunderstood, he says, "Use not vain repetitions." And yet the church has turned right around and made a practice of saying the "Our Fathers" repetitiously, by rote.

Jesus clearly said, "Your Father knows what you need before you ask him" (Matt. 6:8). The implication is, "Why ask?" This leads to one of the most challenging points in the entire prayer process: Don't ask . . . claim your good. Affirm the truth. God, the whole of God-mind, is ever present. God is always centered in you. You need to become centered in God.

Now the question might be asked, and it should be, "If prayer is a science, then why isn't my prayer always answered?" This is like asking, "If there is a principle of electrical energy, why doesn't the light come on every time I throw the switch?" But what if the bulb is burned out? Or there is a break in the circuit? Or the appliance is unplugged? We are told, "Before they call I will answer." In an orderly universe, the need and its answer are always one. We live and move and have our being in infinite mind, a veritable "mind field." In the transcendence of mind, the answer to any need is present and follows as does four from two plus two.

This is what I call "your cosmic counterpart." It is very much like a mystical shadow. There is a whole of you that is present in the energy field that you are, even in a partial expression of you. There is an allness even within illness, an all-sufficiency in any seeming insufficiency.

This does not mean that the answer to your need lies in some divine will separate and apart from your interests. When Jesus says, "Thy Kingdom come, thy will be done," the Kingdom is your potential for fulfillment, and the will is the cosmic force working to reveal it. However, it is an extension of you, not some heavenly plan being forced upon you. It is your truth, your reality, your wholeness.

Prayer is always answered, but the answer, like the results of a scientific experiment, will depend not on what you are hoping to achieve but on the laws governing the elements you have put together. You may be praying for prosperity but combining prayer with the attitudes that make for poverty. You may be seeking healing through spiritual means, and yet you may be combining this with the attitudes that make for illness.

Again, all prayer is answered, though the answer may be accepted at the level of your consciousness. "According to your faith be it done unto you." You see, in prayer we are always dealing with consciousness, and not with some miracle-attempt to bypass it. You may be thinking, "I have been studying truth, and I know that I am where I am because of my consciousness, but I am hoping that God will lift me out of my dilemma and help or heal me."

But God can do no more for you than he can do through you. There is a cosmic counterpart to your need that is perfect, and within you is the unborn possibility to release it. But, as an employer once noted in a memo that was affixed to the paycheck of a worker, "We have decided on a nice salary increase for you, which will become effective when you do."

In other words, God can't lift you out of the gutter. For your in-the-gutter experience is your self-definition at this time. But you can get out of the gutter when you begin to think

49

out-of-the-gutter thoughts. There is a better life for you, but it is not something that will be bestowed on you when you get in the divine favor. It is yours to unfold when you are willing to start earning the right to have it.

You may have an urgent need for guidance, and you may hunger for someone, perhaps divine mind, to tell you what to do, where to go, how to choose. Emerson says, "There is guidance for each one of us, and by lowly listening we will hear the right word."[1] But, you see, guidance is not a specific word of direction. It is a principle of the ever-presence of divine knowingness. "Lowly listening" implies tuning into your own cosmic flow within. It is not a predestined way for you to go, or something God insists that you do whether or not you want it.

God's guidance is the imminence of divine mind that is present in its entirety at every point in space at the same time. So guidance, the clear direction in whatever you may be doing, is always present, and the important decisions are not to be made but to be discovered. Divine guidance is never prejudiced, a pre-determination of what you should do or the way which you should go. It will always relate to your ideals at the highest level of your consciousness. Seeking guidance is not waiting for some answer or help from the outside. It is waiting for an intuitive flash, and then "moving your feet."

A woman visiting friends in the country decided to take a walk in the woods to "commune with nature." She was thrilled with an experience that is normally denied to urban dwellers. Engrossed with the profound sense of involvement in the sight and sound and smell of the beautiful scene, she walked farther

into the woods than she had intended, and she became hope-
lessly lost. She wandered aimlessly for hours, seeking some object to remind her of the way she had come. In desperation she
sat down under a tree and had a fervent prayer experience,
asking God to lead her out of the forest. Several days later she
was discussing the subject of prayer at a bridge-party. She in-
sisted that there was nothing to prayer, telling the ladies of
when she prayed for guidance without results. One woman said,
"You say your prayer was not answered, but you are here, so you
did get out." "Oh yes, I got out, but only because a hunter
came along and found me. I might still be there if I had waited
for God to answer my prayer."

But this is the way prayer works in ninety-nine out of a
hundred cases. The reason for the widespread ineffectuality of
prayer is that prayer is thought of as something outside of consciousness, separate from the intellect, bypassing the mind, a
vague attempt to deal with the "man upstairs," or with some
power outside ourselves.

Now, let us consider what we might call "the equipment of
prayer." The traditional view of prayer might call for . . . a
cathedral, a clergyman (priest, minister, or rabbi), a prayer rug,
a set of rosary beads, a holy communion or mass. However,
there are times when such things are not available. In World
War II there was a slogan, "There are no atheists in fox-holes."
One of the great freedoms experienced through truth is that
you find God at the center of your being, and you bring that
consciousness with you to the religious meeting. An evangelist
may cry out with emotion, "The Holy Spirit is here tonight."

But what he does not say (or even know) is that the Spirit is present because the people are present. The message that should be given to those people as they go forth into lives of challenge is, "Wherever you are, God is."

A little boy was separated from his scout pack. The rest of the scouts searched for him for hours, eventually notifying the police, who called on the community to join in the search. After he had spent a night in what most persons would consider to be a frightening experience, the boy was found, sitting under a tree, calmly whittling with his scout knife. He was asked, "Weren't you afraid, out here in this lonely place all night?" He replied, "Naw, I wasn't afraid. God is here." He was asked, "But how do you know God is here?" "Because I am here." At that moment he had the insight of the presence of God and of his oneness. He may lose it when in Sunday school they deal with a God of the skies, to whom you pray, and from whom you beg for help. But at that moment he knew, "Wherever I am, God is . . . and I AM."

We might consider prayer "equipment" of a more personal kind: such as hands to fold, knees to bend, head to bow, a voice to speak. But amputees or crippled persons who cannot fold their hands or drop to their knees or even bow their heads can still pray effectively. And a mute is not restricted because he or she cannot voice his or her prayer in words.

Thus, the only equipment involved in prayer is that which you have wherever you may be: your mind. As Charles Fillmore says, "The mind is the connecting link between God and oneself."[2] Actually there is a sense in which you do not have a mind. What you call your mind is actually a state of consciousness within divine mind. Your consciousness may identify you on and with various levels within divine mind. As Emerson says, "Prayer is the contemplation of the facts of life from the highest point of view."[3] In other words, prayer is lifting up your self-identification to a higher awareness.

Sometimes we may delude ourselves that we can leave our confused mental state and enter the sanctuary of prayer to solicit divine aid. But you cannot run away from yourself. You can only be transformed by the renewing of your mind. In other words, if you want to pray for peace, you must be willing to get into a peaceful consciousness. If you pray for love, you will be "praying amiss" if you do not get into a loving consciousness. Prayer does not relieve you from responsibility.

Some persons mistakenly think of prayer as a kind of pushing a button: "Dear God, da-da-da-da . . . Amen." Then they are inclined to pray (or think), "Well, I prayed; I sure hope it works." But again, prayer is not something you do. Prayer works according to and within your own consciousness. It can be a strengthening means of lifting you in consciousness, but the effect will be determined by the level of your awareness.

Let's think more about "divine mind." We have tended to think of it as a place in space, something you find and get into. An effective way to understand it is through what I call the "unity principle": Wherever divine mind is, the whole of it must be, and because divine mind is omnipresent, the whole of divine mind must be present in its entirety at every point in space at the same time. Think about that!

We may think of getting an idea out of divine mind. But every idea contains the whole of divine mind within it. So the "all-potential mind" is always present as your capacity to learn, to know. This is why education is not putting knowledge into the mind, but it is progressively tapping into divine mind and releasing it from within you into your experience. Now perhaps you can grasp the meaning of "There is a spirit in man and the inspiration of the almighty giveth him understanding" (Job 32:8).

Perhaps you are meeting a problem, a relationship conflict, a financial crisis, or a computer "glitch." In your cosmic counterpart there is an answer. What you need is to be still and know this, to have faith in the infinite process. Answers will be revealed, right answers, answers that may never have come into your mind before . . . if you can believe.

Thus, the object of prayer is to expand your awareness of infinite mind, which is present where you are. And again, you must unlearn the old thought of prayer as reaching out, reaching up, and appealing, "Dear Lord!" God doesn't want your words of prayer. God doesn't require formal rituals. God doesn't care if you are on your knees or on your toes, sitting up or lying down. The key is to know your oneness, and ideas will come "rushing, streaming, and pouring into you from all sides, while you stand quiet."[4] It is a process that works.

There is much confusion on this point in the teachings of truth. Perceptions differ from teacher to teacher. Not knowing that the mind is a consciousness within infinite mind, some teachers put the focus on programming the mind with positive thoughts. The mind is treated like a "servo-mechanism," as Maxwell Maltz refers to it. It is an attempt to restructure the mind by feeding it like a computer with certain phrases and attitudes. However, while there may be some good results from "mind programming," there may be a frustration of your own flow of transcendence. According to several modern translations of Romans 12:2, Paul wisely says, "Don't let the world squeeze you into its own mold, but let God remold your mind from within."

This "within" that Paul refers to is not some vague and mystical thing. It is just as real as the subconscious mind. It is a phase of mind that is often overlooked, and much of the effort of metaphysics is directed toward the subconscious mind, auto-suggestion, and mind-programming. But you see, Paul is referring to the super-conscious mind. It is the whole of divine mind at the point of oneness with your mind. Jesus called it "the father within who knows your needs . . . and whose good pleasure it is to give you the Kingdom." It is the Christ-mind, the God-self of you that is always present, always active, always seeking to fulfill itself in you. Yes, it is the universe calling you.

It is helpful, too, to see this divine mind counterpart in terms of healing. Paul says, "Not discerning the Lord's body . . . many among you are weak and sickly" (1 Cor. 11:29, 30, KJV). We have been taught that this refers to Jesus' body. But the Lord's body is the Christ body. It is your spiritual-counterpart body. When we were told that we are created in God's image-likeness, it means that there is a pattern within each of us of perfect wholeness, which is being outpictured in the human form according to our level of awareness. Always the healing potential is present, for the divine mind counterpart is always present. We need to turn away from the appearance of a sickly condition and become centered in the awareness of the Lord's body, the law of our wholeness. If we can get this realization clearly enough, a healing activity must follow. If the connections are all good and the light bulb is new, when we throw the switch we will get light. "Then shall the light break forth as the morning, and thy health shall spring forth speedily" (Isa. 58:8, ASV). This is the basis of spiritual healing. But it doesn't work as long as you think of healing as something that has to be done to you or for you. Healing is simply the releasing of the divine potential that is always present.

One of the exciting things about the superconscious mind, the divine mind at the point of your mind, and ever-present and ever-active . . . is its amazing capacity to "remember" things it has never before known. It is what the Bible refers to as "the call to remembrance." All knowledge accrued by humans has come from somewhere. Someone has an idea, possibly a continuity of ideas. Then that person may assemble them together in the form of a textbook. Now we may go to the book to get answers. The accumulated knowledge of civilization in the libraries of the world is a treasured resource. But "the wisdom of this world is folly with God" (1 Cor. 3:19). The wisdom of the world created the cliché "reaching for the moon" as a symbol of the impossible. But someone had an idea, which gave birth to many other ideas . . . and the impossible became possible and was achieved. Thus, if you can imagine something, you have touched an idea in divine mind. If you keep open to the inner flow, and "trust the process," then it is certainly possible of achievement . . . and there is no limit.

I believe it was Emerson who said that man is an inlet who may become an outlet to all there is in God. This shows what a tremendously endowed creature you are. It shows that there is no limit to what can happen as you become more and more aware of the presence, more and more conditioned to the divine mind counterpart, and let the process unfold.

So, prayer is a supermind process. It does not reach out and up to God for help, but seeks to get centered at the supermind level within. Jesus says, "Enter into the inner chamber . . . " and let the process work.

Typically, we are all too impatient. We may have an idea of what we want to do, and we pray about it. We may even say we are praying for guidance in the matter. But if truth is known, we are really praying for a divine approval of something we have already made up our mind to do, whether we get the approval or not. This is not prayer, it is playing games.

The important thing is to realize that, "I of myself can do nothing." I may have a plan, but only the creative flow of divine mind can perfect it. It is well to remember that there is a cosmic counterpart to the plan in infinite mind, which is sensed in the inspiration that formed the plan. I must take time every day and often through the day to listen in conscious receptivity to the inner directions for working out the plan to completion.

There is a story about Beethoven that I have used for years, an apocryphal story I have been unable to locate. It tells how Beethoven had a flash of inspiration that came to his mind like one great chord, "hummmh." And just like that he heard an entire symphony. It took him weeks to get it on paper, and today it takes the better part of an hour for an orchestra to play it. But Beethoven caught it in a flash. However, in a little book by Walter Abell, *Talks with Great Composers*, he gives anecdotes of a similar nature about Brahms, Wagner, Puccini, and others. Abell quotes Brahms as saying, "I always contemplate my oneness with the Creator before commencing to compose. I immediately feel vibrations that thrill my whole being. . . . I see clearly what is obscure in my ordinary mode. . . . Straightway the idea flows in upon me. . . . Measure by measure, the finished product is revealed."[5] Where does this creative input come from? It comes out of the God-potential within. Symphonic works were the way Brahms (and Beethoven) caught the inspiration. To Michelangelo it may have come as "the Boy David." To a Madison Avenue executive it could come as a detailed advertising program for the introduction of a new product.

The true prayer is the supermind process. And the divine mind counterpart within is the answer present even before we call. And you are never further away from your answer to the most complicated challenge than the flow in mind of one idea.

"In the twinkling of an eye I will come." We have been told that this meant Jesus will come. But Jesus is talking about the supermind awareness, your cosmic counterpart answer. As fast as you can snap your fingers, you can receive an answer, a whole symphony in one chord, the details for a revolutionary invention in one equation, or the plot of a new novel in one illumined sentence.

My beautiful helpmate and I have a secret understanding about this. If she sees me struggling over some article or lesson or radio talk, she will just put her head in the door of my study and snap her fingers. And I snap my fingers to indicate that I catch the reminder. It is all we have to "say." It is a gentle reminder that the answer is within, a cosmic counterpart that contains limitless words and descriptive phrases that will flow forth effortlessly if I can acknowledge the process and believe that it can be done.

This is prayer at its finest. But it is not something you do to God. It is an acknowledgment of the ever-presence of the divine activity, and then, "moving your feet," getting on with your work, knowing that you are in the unimpeded flow of the creative process.

This is not turning to God to inform him of your need. It is getting still, centering yourself at the "still point" within, knowing that the answer is present in divine mind. In the same sense, the potential for healing or for remission of a dread illness is always present within you. Your prayer is to acknowledge it and rest in that consciousness. And then to move your feet in the direction of the goal that you have envisioned.

Remember, there is nowhere to go in prayer, for God is present, the whole of divine mind is present, and the answer to any and every need is present in the cosmic counterpart within. The universe is calling. Are you listening?

CHAPTER 6

Relax, Let Go, Let God

One of the most important errors to be unlearned is the idea that religion is a thing in itself, something you pick up or lay down, something you subscribe to or a church you join, something you study and memorize by rote . . . and along with that, the idea that prayer is a pre-scribed ritual, like the grand ceremonies of a lodge. We have handed down religious teachings as ready-made, cut-and-dried propositions. I call them "custom-made convictions."

As part of this scenario, truth is given as infallible. There is nothing more to be said. There is nothing to do but believe it. All through our lives, instead of pursuing the spiritual quest and working toward truth, we simply work from truth, or what we have been told is truth.

But an infallible standard is a temptation to have a me-chanical faith. Thus, we have tended to make one great act of faith, and then have done with it. We are saved . . . we join the church . . . it's all over. This has left us with imposing temples and cathedrals with gaudy interiors. God is somewhere in back of the altar, dispensed in small portions by priests, ministers, and rabbis. No doubt many of us have cried out with Emerson, "Why can't we have a first-hand and immediate experience with God?" Thus, in this study we are dealing with prayer, not as a religious act or a theological exercise, but as a personal experience of oneness, something that we do, not for God, but in and for ourselves, something we do to lift ourselves to a transcendental awareness of God.

We might say that prayer is a gesture, a personally symbolic act. But what does it mean? We make many gestures. Consider the gesture of extending the hand in friendship to a stranger. Originally this meant to show that you were unarmed, that you came in peace. People took each other's hand in a bargain that they would not harm one another. Of course, today, most handshakes are mere formalities.

Consider the folded hands of prayer. It is a lovely symbol depicted by artists to connote piety. But what does the gesture really mean? To many persons it is a sign of entreaty, a gesture of begging, pleading, interceding. But actually, the folded hands together, throughout the many religions of the world, imply unity, a sense of wholeness. It is the oriental *namaskar*, the divinity within me that salutes the divinity within you.

It is important, however, to get the awareness that the gesture of prayer is not directed toward anyone or anything outside of oneself. To repeat, prayer is not something you do for God. Your words are not for God's ears. Your gestures are not for his eyes. "Your Father knoweth what things you have need of before you ask Him" (Matt. 6:8, ASV). In the gesture, the words, the form, whatever else your prayer involves, you are seeking to realize your wholeness, your transcendence.

We will say again, and we will repeat it over and over throughout this discourse, prayer is not conditioning God to your needs, but conditioning your needs to the activity of God. We don't want to seem repetitious, but it is vital that you catch this point. Prayer is not trying to reach God, or inform God, or tell God all about your troubles. It is to know God as the infinite resource within, and to expand your self-realization.

Challenge yourself to become aware of the presence of God. One truth teacher adds confusion, rather than clarity, when, in describing the effects of prayer, he says (and he says it often), "When you get the awareness of truth and speak the healing word . . . Pop!—God comes in." But God doesn't come in, for God never went out. When you pray, God doesn't go anywhere or come from anywhere. And you don't go anywhere. You simply remove the blinders from your eyes. You become aware that you are an expression of God, and that God is a deeper dimension of yourself expressing himself *as* you. There is no need to bargain with God, to coax a reluctant God to work a miracle on your behalf. If this is your purpose, then, as Jesus told his disciples, "You ask wrong" (James 4:6). God knows your needs, and God is the answer. As Tennyson so aptly puts it, "Closer is he than breathing, and nearer than hands and feet."[1]

What you need is to forget how worried and confused you are, and remember how wonderful you are. Does that surprise you? It certainly goes against the traditional prayer attitude that you are a miserable sinner. It is interesting that the root word from which *prayer* is derived is *pal-al,* from the ancient Sanskrit, which literally means "judging oneself to be wondrously made." A new horizon opens to those who begin to think of prayer as knowing how wonderful they are, how creative, how at one with the divine flow.

So you see, true prayer is esentially wrapped up in the psalmist's call to "Be still and know that I am God" (Ps. 46:10). This is really what it is all about. How simple! Yet we make it so complex. The first step is to relax the involuntary tensions of the mind, and lift your thoughts to synchronize with the steady flow of transcendence . . . to affirm how wonderful you are, how beautifully you are created.

Now again, here is your reminder: God can do no more for you than he can do through you. There is no way that your prayer can be answered unless you change the level of your thinking. Paul says "Be transformed by the renewal of your mind" (Rom. 12:2). The root of this phrase in the Greek is the word *metanoia*—literally meaning, "to think differently." In short, if you want to be healthy, you must stop thinking of yourself as sick. If you want to be prosperous and successful, you must renounce the practice of thinking of yourself as a failure.

Now, make no mistake about it, this is not easy. It calls for a disciplined effort to let go of attachments to the past, to clear out of the mind the prejudices, the pessimism, the self-pity . . . to renounce gripes, grudges, and grouches . . . to relinquish all hates and hurts, all false beliefs and foolish fears, all ideas of lack and limitation. Traditional medicine may do a pretty good job of curing your symptoms, but you can only be healed causally by making a concerted effort at mental house-cleaning . . . then consciously letting go, and letting God. The words *cure* and *healing* are used in this way purposely. An aspirin may cure a headache. But healing can only come through the release of tension and by dissolving the attitudes or emotions that are responsible for the tension.

In the early days of the American Revolution, one man was overcome with fear that the British army would overrun his village and subject it to unspeakable indignities. He wisely secreted a boat at the river, hiding it on the bank near some bulrushes, and one night he heard the frantic cry, "The British are coming!" According to his carefully formulated plan, he dashed out of his house, ran to the river, and jumped into his boat. There seemed to be a strong current, but he rowed confidently, feeling smug about his preparedness. It was a dark and foggy night. He rowed all night until exhaustion set in. Then, as the sun rose and the fog lifted, he suddenly became aware that he was right where he had started, for he had forgotten to cut the boat free from its mooring.

It is an important lesson. You can't have a harmonious relationship and hold onto your resentment, too. You can't hold onto your anger and bitterness and still have a healthy heart and a settled stomach. Jesus makes it very clear that you can't expect God to help you or heal you unless you make room for the answer to your prayers by letting go of your negative feelings. He says, "If you come to the altar with your gift [symbolizing your prayer effort], and there remember that your brother has aught against you [and perhaps you have aught against your brother], leave there the gift, and go and be reconciled with your brother, and then come and offer your gift" (Matt. 5:23, 24). In other words, if you are blocking the flow of life or substance or love by your resentment or unforgiveness, not even God can break through with the good you desire. That may shock you, to hear that there is something God cannot do. For haven't we been told that God can do all things? But you see, God is not someone who works on you from the outside. God is the dynamic potential of your being . . . and again, God can do no more for you than he can do through you.

Emmet Fox says,

> When you hold resentment against anyone, you are
> bound to that person by a cosmic link—a really rough
> metal chain. You are tied by a cosmic tie to the very thing
> you hate. The thing you hate is inexorably a part of your
> consciousness. The one person in the whole world whom
> you most dislike is the very one to whom you are attach-
> ing yourself by a hook that is stronger than steel.[2]

And don't delude yourself that when you pray, you bypass all this and achieve God's forgiveness. In the Lord's Prayer, Jesus says, "Forgive us our debts as we also have forgiven our debtors." God forgives as we forgive. But that is not entirely correct, for God doesn't really forgive . . . because there is no unforgiveness in him. God is love. And through the attitude of forgiveness we open ourselves to that love. Love is always and eternally present, but we block it with our resistance. Jesus' statement is like saying, "The sun comes streaming in the window when we raise the blinds." But of course we know that the sun doesn't really come in. It simply shines, and we accept the light and warmth as we eliminate the barrier.

There is a tendency to rush pell-mell into prayer without adequate preparation. Like the man with his escape boat, we neglect to cut ourselves free from that which binds. Let go! This is the first step in scientific prayer. There are three important steps which we will outline in this chapter and the next two. The second step is going within to experience your oneness with infinite power in a process called *meditation* or *the silence.* And the third step is the projection of that power through affirmation of truth or spiritual treatment.

The interesting thing is that many times, just in the process of letting go, we open the answering flow immediately, and the problem is solved or the condition healed, with no further prayer effort required. As we pointed out earlier, there is a cosmic counterpart in infinite mind to every human need, along with a desire to fill that need. The confusion of praying to God in prayer-book language and a pleading tone is normally counterproductive, serving to block the flow rather than to open the way to prayer's answer.

There is an old-time religious hymn, "Take it to the Lord in prayer." Take all your troubles, your woes, your anxieties, to God, we were told by the preachers. However, when we catch the idea and the feeling of the transcendent nature of God, a new and startling realization dawns: "Don't take it to the Lord at all!" God doesn't want your negatives. God is light, and in that light there can be no darkness of limitation. We are told, "Thou art of purer eyes than to behold evil . . . " (Hab. 1:13, KJV). It may be helpful to take inventory of your needs, even to make a list of the "troubles I've seen." This list, however, is not for God, but to remind you of what you are holding onto. Once the list is complete, then its purpose has been fulfilled. Lay it aside. Better yet, put it into the fireplace, where it will be consumed. Watch the paper be swallowed up in flames. Get the sense of freedom, as you consciously let go. Now you are ready to let God.

Jesus said, "Do not judge by appearances, but judge with righteous judgment" (John 7:24). A technique for dealing with appearances, as suggested by Emilie Cady in her classic work *Lessons in Truth,* is denial. "There is no absence of life, substance, or intelligence anywhere." "There are no God-empty spots." "I have no fear."[3] These are sample denials. By making statements like these, you tend to correct your perspective, seeing beyond the appearance. However, there is a lot of confusion about this. To deny a thing does not mean to refuse to deal with it. Rather, it is the most effective way of dealing with it. When you have a problem, don't say "there is no problem," but rather "there are no unanswerable problems." You are denying that the appearance tells the whole story, so *you* tell the whole story, which is the basis of an affirmation or treatment. The denial is a letting go of the shackles of limitation.

The interesting thing is that when you have a concern over some difficulty which has caused you to pray about it, you approach your prayer with a built-in anxiety or tension. Thus, the very first step in the science of prayer is the conscious act of letting go. If you begin your prayer with a judgment about the severity of the problem, you are saying, in effect, "Boy, this is going to be a difficult one." You may clench your fists and tense your body. It will be very much like driving with the brakes on.

So, settle with this attitude of hopelessness. Deny it, let it go. Prayer is no time for physical tension. If your hands are taut, that is a good signal that you need to let go. You may say, "I have prayed all night about this problem." But you are deluding yourself. That was not prayer. You were holding onto the problem all night. You may have commenced your prayer with "Dear Lord" and concluded it with "Amen"—but you probably had an orgy of worry and self-pity in between. Let go . . . and let God. "It is your Father's good pleasure to give you the Kingdom" (Luke 12:32). The whole universe is conspiring to establish you in health and harmony. Let go and let it unfold. The universe is calling you to wholeness.

Prayer does not make answers. It simply accepts answers that are always within. "Before they call I will answer" (Isa. 65:24). Prayer is not an attempt to "get through to God," to get your requests on the spindle on his desk, so to speak. This is not what prayer is about. The need is to relax the involuntary tensions of the mind, and to let go and give way to the life and substance of spirit. It is not as much a thing to do, as it is a thing to let be done.

Relax, let go, and let God! We say the words so easily. But we must realize that it is a depth uncovered. Just relax and let go. God, the creative flow, is realized in you. Just let it happen. If you keep emphasizing how terrible things are, how bad you feel, how much you hurt, there will be no help, no communion, no awakening to the flow. Prayer is centering your attention on the truth of wholeness.

This may well be your biggest problem: not the conditions or persons that are harassing you, but your tendency to hold onto them. Freedom calls for a dramatic act of letting go. Here is an illustration that may help you to get the picture.

An interesting system has been used for capturing monkeys in the jungles of Africa. The goal is to take the monkeys alive and unharmed for shipment to the zoos of America. In an extremely humane way, the captors use heavy bottles, with long narrow necks, into which they deposit a handful of sweet-smelling nuts. The bottles are dropped on the jungle floor, and the captors return the next morning to find a monkey trapped next to each bottle. How is it accomplished? The monkey, attracted by the aromatic scent of the nuts, comes to investigate the bottle, puts its arm down the long narrow neck, closes its hand around the nuts, and is trapped. The monkey can't take its hand out of the bottle as long as it's holding the nuts, but it is unwilling to open its hand and let them go. The bottle is too heavy to carry away . . . so the monkey is trapped.

We may smile at the foolish monkeys . . . but how often we hold to our problems as tenaciously as the monkeys hold to the nuts in the bottle. And so, figuratively we carry our bottle around with us, feeling very sorry for ourselves, and begging for sympathy from others, even from God.

I may go to see an analyst or a spiritual counselor, dragging my bottle with me. I take my seat, lifting the bottle onto my lap, and say, "I have this problem, see!" The counselor tries to help correct my thinking, and possibly, we conclude the interview with a time of prayer. I express appreciation, saying I have been helped, then I pick up my bottle and leave, dragging the bottle behind me. All the counseling in the world cannot help me until I let go of the nuts. I may complain that the problem is with people or conditions, "the way people treat me at work," or "they fired me without notice." But in every case, the trouble is not what happened to me. It is what I am doing about what is happening in me.

We are told, "God hath made man upright, but they have sought out many inventions" (Eccles. 7:29, KJV). God made the monkey to climb and run free, but the monkey decided to clasp its hands on the nuts, and it was trapped. God made you whole and healthy, but in some way beyond your conscious awareness, you may have frustrated the divine flow, and thus you may be holding onto your problem. You will not let it go. The monkey was always a free monkey, but it was bound by its failure to understand itself. At any time, it had the power to say to its hand, "Open!" And you have the power to say to yourself, "I let go of fear and worry and resentment and regret.

71

I let it all go." Thus, at any time you feel that you are acting like a monkey, you have the power to give way, to let go, and let flow.

Here is an imaging exercise for you to work with: Take another inventory, listing all the challenges, conflicts and difficulties that you may have. Let them be symbolized by the nuts in the bottle with the long, narrow neck. Feel your hand clasping a nut. Feel the frustration and pain of entrapment. Ask yourself, "Am I content to have this bottle? Do I really want to be free?" There is only one way. Open your hand and feel your arm slipping out of the bottle. You are free. You might say, "I let go of resistance, resentment, and anxiety." Let it all go. There is no way to gain freedom unless you let go. Even God cannot set you free unless you follow the freeing call to let go. Face forward and let go!

Relaxation is a vital step in getting into a prayer consciousness. It is the first step in scientific prayer. Prayer is not a physical activity, but if we are trapped in a body-consciousness, our way is effectively blocked.

It is important to establish yourself in the feeling of dominion. You are not your body. You *have* a body. And the you that has the body has the power to master the body. Here is an exercise for establishing the feeling of dominion. Tell your right arm to rise . . . and then to fall. Then the left arm—rise . . . fall. It is one of the greatest lessons you can learn, and so very simple. Can you sense the impact? You see, you *can* control your body. You are in charge.

Now, have a drill in relaxation as training in a vital preparation for prayer. Sit in a chair, feet flat on the floor, body erect. Tell your hands to relax . . . let them drop loosely in your lap. Then, working progressively from the top of your head to the tip of your toes, go through all the parts of your body (your forehead, your eyes, nose, mouth, chin, neck, etc.), saying in order, "Relax, and let go!" Eventually get the sense that your body is as limp as a dishrag, falling in a heap on the floor. Just rest in that state long enough to feel a sense of dominion over the tensions of the body, and a symbolic sense of freedom over the anxieties and frustrations of the mind.

If you are still enough, in mind and body, you experience the inspiration of the Almighty, saying to you figuratively if not actually, "You are my beloved child. You are loved. You are free. You are whole. You are creative. You are successful." Remember, "It is your Father's good pleasure to give you the Kingdom" (Luke 12:32). The activity of God is always seeking to heal you, to bless you, to fill all your vessels with good. When you get yourself out of the way, the divine flow does its perfect work. However, it is not that you stir God to activity. You simply become receptive to the divine activity that is always present as a presence. It might be good to emphasize the connection between the words *present* and *presence*. The presence of God is present, ever-present, omnipresent. The *presence* can never be absent, though at times *we* may be absent in consciousness. As Emerson says, if we can get away from the preconceived anthropomorphic notions, really break their hold on our mind, then God fires us with his presence. The words of Meister Eckhart speak dynamically to our need to let go as the basic step in the process of scientific prayer: "God expects but one thing of you, and that is that you should come out of yourself insofar as you are a created being, and *let* God *be* God in you."[4]

CHAPTER 7

The Way of the Silence

As we have said, getting a new insight in scientific prayer calls for unlearning many attitudes and practices that we have become conditioned to over many years. These changes do not come easily. We are faced with the need to perceive a larger thought of God, which may be as difficult as the mental adjustment required of the people of Columbus' day, after he had proved the world to be round. It was actually several hundred years before people could see a sunrise or sunset without perceiving a flat world. And today we can never take for granted that we have disposed of the "God out there" perception, and totally established ourselves in the "presence."

So, to repeat, prayer is not trying to reach for God, not even to reach God. It is giving up the very desire to reach. We have talked about praying *to* God, sending our appeal to the "man upstairs." In this context, our prayer is a performance that we put on for his eyes and ears. However, if we can just get the perspective of the presence, then God is not someone to pray *to*, but a depth of awareness and energy to pray *from*. Thus, a vital step in prayer is focusing on that depth.

The religious student of the Western world has been strongly conditioned to religious dualism, the perception of God *and* humanity. Thus, we Westerners have found it extremely difficult to understand the oriental concept of monism—the awareness of one basic spirit, one mind, one life substance. Thus, though in recent times there has been a widespread interest in the Eastern practice of meditation, in most cases it has been taken out of the context of the oneness of God and humanity. The emphasis has been instead upon "consciousness expansion," upon "relaxation response." These are extremely helpful states, but they can never lead a person to true self-awareness. This can only come through "practicing the presence," or the realization of oneness with the ever-present divine flow.

The word *meditation* conjures up the image of a scantily clad guru sitting cross-legged on a chaise, perhaps holding a bouquet of flowers in his hands. It is not surprising that most clergymen reject meditation as a heretical practice, because it has come from what they refer to as "pagan religions of the East." Obviously, it meets with resistance because it turns a person away from dependence on dogma, ritual, and clergy intermediaries. Thus, it is a threat to the religious establishment.

However, "the inward art," as Bradford calls meditation, is an emphasis on turning within, touching the depths of your inner self: the point where God is manifesting *as* you. It is a vital step in prayer that has its roots, for the Western seeker, in Jesus' call to "enter into thine inner chamber, and having shut the door, pray to the Father in secret . . . " (Matt. 6:6, ASV). It is the absence of this meditation process that has been the missing key to power in the whole Judeo-Christian concept of prayer. Thus, the prayer of institutional religion has deteriorated into a performance of words, form, and ritual . . . with little or no real communion, no silence, no listening.

We are suggesting three basic steps or stages in the process of scientific prayer: (1) Relax and let go. (2) Turn inward to become one with the secret power. (3) Project this power with an affirmation or treatment. This last step will be dealt with in the next chapter.

Imagine, if you will, a nineteenth-century fire department. Firefighting often consisted of forming bucket brigades between a source of water and the fire. Buckets of water would be filled from a well or stream and passed on by means of a human chain, with the last person in the chain throwing the buckets of water onto the fire. It was a crude but often effective system. But just imagine the buckets being passed on through the human chain without having first been dipped in the water. How foolish the last person would feel as they threw their "buckets of nothing" onto the fire! And so it is with prayer that consists of rattling off words, without taking time to touch the inner "wellspring of living water."

Meditation has become a popular word in the past thirty years. But it has been a confused term. It has been thought of as a thing. One may say, "Oh yes, I meditate." Or, "No, I don't meditate, but I would like to learn. . . . Tell me how." And right at this point we become vulnerable to all kinds of delusion, because of the many different ways that exist. Of course the person we're asking gives their particular way authoritatively as "the" way.

The great yoga master Aurobindo said that it is not necessary to be told how to meditate. He held that whatever you need will come of itself, if in your practice and at all times you are sincere and keep yourself open to the divine force. This should be considered by all those who have "gotten into meditation." It is an important insight, suggesting that you are a part of a wholeness which is God. So there is nowhere to go in meditation. It is not trying to get into something or out of something or up to something. And it is not trying to *do* something. Actually it is *not doing*.

Meditation, thus, is not a thing you learn to do, for the *how* involves a technique, which may be mechanical; and there is simply no way that you can experience oneness in a mechanical way. You don't need to know how. You need only to desire. God is seeking you. One woman had a naively brilliant realization. She said, "Aha, now I see, God is praying for me." When you let go and become open and receptive, the divine flow springs forth speedily.

I prefer to use the term *the silence* instead of *meditation*, for it puts the emphasis on a state of consciousness, instead of a mental exercise. Jesus says, "Go into your room and shut the door, . . . and in praying, do not heap up empty phrases . . . " (Matt. 6:6–7). In other words, "wordless silence."

Normally, prayer is chiefly concerned with words—whether spontaneous words or those taken out of a prayer book. With these the average person "says their prayers." I often say that learning is what remains when you have forgotten everything you have heard. In this same sense, prayer is what you experience beyond the words that you repeat. If you don't experience anything beyond the words, then you may not be really praying. You are just mumbling words and mouthing propositions. This is not the high-level prayer we are talking about. Prayer is where you are in consciousness.

From the wisdom of ancient China there is a saying that if a person be absolutely quiet, the heavenly heart will manifest itself. To be absolutely quiet! This is not easy, for most of us are so conditioned to activity and noise that silence is deafening. Like a city person going to the country . . . quiet country lanes, just the rush of the wind through the trees. It is deafening!

Have you been throwing "buckets of nothing" on the flames? Be still! Turn away from the tendency to plunge into prayer by rattling off your repertoire of affirmations. Now in truth we believe in the prayer of affirmation rather than supplication. We speak the word of truth. But unless we become centered in the source of power within, we may use affirmations and treatments like a cosmic club with which we try to beat off the terrors of night and day. We talk of the power of the spoken word, but words have no power of themselves. They are marvelous instruments of power, if we are in tune with the divine flow. Otherwise, when we are working with a problem, there is a tendency to start mouthing affirmations, as if we were throwing darts.

Consider an archer in target practice. The archer stands on the archery line, bow and arrow in hand, facing a target fifty yards in the distance. Now, the object is to send the arrow to the target. The intellect might logically lead one to fling the arrow as far as possible. But you can't fling an arrow more than a few yards. There is certainly no way you could get it to the target in this way. That is why you have a bow. You fix the arrow in the bow, left arm stiff, arrow fixed to the string with the thumb and index finger of your right hand. Then you pull the arrow back, back, back. Your object is to send the arrow to the target, but you are pulling the arrow away from the target. There is a secret process . . . you pull the arrow back as far as you can, building up great latent energy. Then what do you do? Flick the arrow out? No! You simply let it go. That's correct, just let it go. And swoosh, the arrow flies straight and true toward the distant target.

It is a good illustration, explaining the role of the silence in prayer. We want to pray for the condition "out there." But we need to let go . . . and go down our well to experience and become imbued with transcendent energy. Then we may look on the object for which we are praying, and with no anxious effort, simply take our word of truth, let it go, and swoosh, it goes forth to accomplish that whereto it is sent. And now, mystery of mysteries, "The word which you hear is not mine but the Father's who sent me" (John 14:24). It is a reminder that I of myself can do nothing, but through the power of God in me, I can do all things. I have little power in my human consciousness, but when I am lifted up into the Christ-consciousness and attuned to the divine flow, I can do great things.

Within you right now and all the time there is a transcendent power. It is important to take time frequently to be still and get centered at the "still point" within. That is the consciousness level where you are the focus of the limitless energy of the universe.

Many persons complain that they never have original ideas. They say, "Oh, it would be nice to be creative. I really admire creative people, but no inspiration ever comes to me." And I often boldly say, "Why don't you get still and listen?" Often these people are so busy talking, usually about their deficiencies and the injustices rained upon them, that they never really get themselves out of the way so as to experience themselves at the point of oneness. It is as impossible for one who is surrounded with the ceaseless babble of conversation to experience the flow of creative ideas as it is for pure water to flow through a pipe containing crude oil. There is never a moment in your life when the guidance you desire or the creative ideas you need are not present within you, as dynamically present as the force of gravity is present.

The more we know about *homo sapiens*, this person you are, the more we know that you are a cosmic creature with the whole universe concentrated in you. You are potentially the greatest concentration of energy in the world. Through the projection of this energy (which is precisely what prayer is about), you become God in action.

Jesus demonstrated what you can do and be when you concentrate your spiritual energies. He proved that there is always enough power within you to accomplish whatever you need, provided it is constructively applied.

We are dealing with silence as a part of the prayer process. I prefer the term *silence* over *meditation,* for it tends to distinguish the process from the Eastern practice. It is a vital part of prayer, the step of going down the well within to touch the cosmic stream. Again, it is not praying *to* God, but praying *from* the consciousness *of* God. The way of the silence is to plumb the depths within and feel your oneness with God, then project the power toward that which concerns you. You may want to speak some words of truth in a treatment and affirmation. I will say more about this specifically in the next chapter.

One of the most important experiences for all persons is the desire to turn from the confusion of life at the circumference. The prodigal son in the far country "came to himself." He suddenly realized, "I don't belong here. I want to go home. I will arise and go unto my Father." But you see, this did not involve going anywhere in a geographical sense. It was simply a matter of "waking up."

Meister Eckhart went right to the heart of this parable when he commented that the prodigal was in the far country, but the Father was at home. At home in the center of his being. The prodigal in the far country represents living at the circumference of being in sensual and materialistic consciousness. It is the dream-sleep of human consciousness. The prodigal came to himself; he woke up. This is the secret of the silence. We have believed that the root of reality is out there in the world of money, possessions, relationships, and circumstances. We go off in an endless search for the "holy grail" of meaning in our work, in acquisitions, and in getting "turned on" by special persons. But when we "come to ourselves" we realize that the goal is to find it not out there, but within ourselves. The answer is in the way of the silence.

It is a vital step in the prayer process. In our desire to find help in a time of need, our tendency is to commence reciting rote prayers or metaphysical statements. In the science of prayer we are suggesting, first, getting relaxed and receptive, letting go of stress and anxiety. Then, as a second step, before we proceed to speak words of truth, we seek to become established in oneness with the flow of spiritual energy within. This is the place of meditation, or the silence.

The question may be asked, "What do I meditate upon?" But answering this question may give rise to meditating *about* . . . and soon we are meditating about our problems. This serves to emphasize the negative over and over in a veritable orgy of concentrated worry. This is not prayer.

We have pointed out that it is helpful to write out a list of the things that you want to pray about. When you are satisfied that you have accounted for all your concerns, then the list has fulfilled its purpose just in the writing. So, lay it aside, perhaps even burn it up . . . in a symbolic letting go. You see, you should not seek answers in your time of silence. Just draw back the bow, get centered in the cosmic flow.

Human consciousness tends to focus on doing something, but as you let go, you must let go the sense of *doing* . . . and become established in the awareness of *not doing*. Imagine yourself experiencing a great insurgence of energy . . . all the while keeping the mind in an attitude of "don't-give-a-darn-ness."

Take a moment now to have a visualization exercise. Imagine an ocean scene, with the water moving turbulently, and with many great white-capped waves. Now (it is your image so you can deal with it as you will), imagine that you are one of the waves. The wave that is you moves through the ocean. It has body. It has motion. What is this wave that is you? It is the ocean formed at that point into a wave. It is never more nor less than ocean. Now, what is your relationship with God? You are the activity of God expressing *as* you. And you can never be more nor less than God. God is in you as the ocean is in a wave.

See the ocean becoming calm, and the waves becoming smaller. See the whole body of water becoming placid, and eventually becoming smooth as glass. What happened to the wave that is you? It is where it always was and what it always was . . . the ocean expressing at this point as a wave. It is simply a potential, but it is there. And now, see this in your relationship with God. As you become still . . . still . . . still . . . get the sense of losing your desires, your ego, your sometimes turbulent personality. "Be still and know that I am God." Perhaps you have long had trouble in saying, "I am God." But in this context it is easy, isn't it? Think about this!

In the *Bhagavad Gita* we read, "He whose self is established in oneness, whose vision is everywhere, sees the self in all beings, and all beings in the self."[1]

An exercise like this can be helpful in getting out of a problem-consciousness, breaking down the walls that separate and cutting away the loose ends that confuse, getting the sense that there is only God. How long should you rest in this transcendent consciousness? Actually, time is relative. One answer might be, as long as you can hold the image in concentration without stress. It is a recharging process. It depends on how drained you may have been. And remember, this is not something you are doing. Think of a battery being charged. Does it need to have something to do? No! It simply accepts the charge. Just be still and know.

It is good to have a special time and place to engage in your silent time. But you *can* have a silence anywhere at any time. Wherever you may be, you may plug into what the Easterners refer to as "the mother sea of consciousness." In the context of prayer, we want to see the silence, not as its own end, but as a creative way to achieve the greater end of projecting prayer power. However, there is a discipline involved, which can be achieved by practice. It is helpful to have an occasional silent time, just to develop skill in concentrating at the point of oneness.

Don't be deluded into the belief that the silence calls for assuming a special position of the body. Yoga positions may be helpful as an exercise, or as a symbolic gesture, but they most certainly are not necessary.

Meditation "systems" often stress the importance of breathing, and certainly most persons need to learn to breathe more efficiently. But this should not be made into a fetish. It is good to begin the silent time with a few deep breaths, holding the thought that you are breathing in the life and breath of the Almighty, and breathing out all impurities of mind and body. Again, it can be an effective symbolic gesture. I have a simple technique that has been very effective for me. On the inhalation I form the words "God is," and on the exhalation I say, "I am." Breathe normally, but affirm on the breath, "God is . . . I am; God is . . . I am; God is . . . I am." Inhale . . . exhale! Don't make it a mechanical thing. It has little to do with the meditation process, but it can become a symbolic gesture that you can identify with. If you are unable to sleep at night, you can use this exercise to make the sleepless period spiritually productive.

In time, after much practice, you will associate this act of breathing with preparation for a silence, and thus, by drawing a few breaths, you will go right into a state of oneness. A quick drawing of the breath in a time of crisis or emergency can become a symbolic gesture leading to an instant release of the energy of divine protection.

Don't go into a silence expecting to have a conscious experience. Things *may* happen to you and in you. But more often than not, it will simply be an infilling that will give no sensation whatever, just the feeling of well-being. Don't look for ESP or psychic experiences . . . or your subconscious mind may oblige by producing such an experience for you, which may have nothing to do with the spiritual goals of your silence, and may actually mislead you.

Remember, aside from your times of practice, the silence is not an end in itself. It is a means to the end of becoming imbued with power, building a focus of spiritual energy. Then you project this energy as you speak your word of truth. You pull the arrow back, back, back . . . then you let it go in the word of truth. You may simply voice the words "I am," which constitute the most powerful affirmation you can utter. Or you may use the "I am" and "God is" breathing exercise. Or you may use a prayer treatment, such as, "I am a perfect child of God. I am one with divine love and infinite substance. I am in the flow of God's great good that is unfolding for me now."

But remember, you are not just mouthing words. The words you speak become the spirit expressing itself through you. Your words become the channel through which there is an outforming of "answers without ceasing."

True prayer is not indulging in the tensions and frustrations that have led you to engage in the prayer, for this would be extremely counterproductive. Prayer must involve a letting go, a recentering of yourself in oneness with God, and then, instead of praying *to* God about the problem, you pray *from* the consciousness of God, projecting spiritual power in a transcendent flow to heal and harmonize and make you prosper.

In other words, you must get away from the sense of struggling, frantically beating on the doors of heaven, trying desperately to solicit God's help: "O God, I need you now." If God were the anthropomorphic being we tend to relate to him as being, he might say, "All right, if you need me, be still and accept it . . . for my answer was present in you even before you asked for my help. Be still and know . . . "

Be still . . . and the Father who knows what things you have need of will reward you openly. The Kingdom of God is within you, your very own divine potential. Be still . . . accept this transcendent self of you, this spiritual process in you. Trust this process. Its action is wonderful!

CHAPTER 8

Affirmation and Treatment

In this study of the science of prayer we are trying to get a larger thought of God, a new insight into ourselves, and a more expansive awareness of the universe in which we live. If you have been strongly conditioned by a traditional religious perspective, the concept we are suggesting may be shocking and disturbing. And if this is the case, good! It is my hope that it will be a shock of unlearning, leading to an enthusiastic "Aha!" Emerson suggests that when you break with the God of tradition and destroy the God of the intellect, God will fire you with his presence. Seriously, we are suggesting that you take God down out of the skies, and begin to relate to true omnipresence and omnipotence. It is an important breakthrough in consciousness wherein you let go of the God "out there," and "let God be God in you."

You see, in the traditional view, God is the dispenser of things from his heavenly storehouse. Even wise and sophisticated people change their character in prayer, putting on the costume and the tin cup of the beggar. So, if there is a need for supply, they pray to God for money. If the need is for healing, they ask God for health. But the new insight in truth, continuing to shock, says that God doesn't *have* substance, God *is* substance. God doesn't *have* life, God *is* life. When Jesus said, "The kingdom of God is within you," he was saying that every thing that you might need in life exists as a potentiality within you now. Thus the need is not to pray for things, but to become a channel for the release of that cosmic energy that takes form *as* the things. Claim your good and become a positive channel for its release. This is the purpose of affirmation and treatment.

The eternal question is, "Why wasn't my prayer answered?" This discouraged cry leads to foolish attempts to explain, with clichés such as, "It is God's will," and "God is punishing you for your sins." But you see, there are some things that even an omnipotent God cannot do. One of them is to work in opposition to his own laws. For there is a science of prayer, even as there is a science of chemistry and mathematics. We do not pray to the science of chemistry to make combinations of elements that cannot be combined. And who would ask the science of mathematics to support or justify a false calculation? This is not to minimize the power of prayer, any more than we would minimize the power of electricity. However, prayer, like electricity, must be properly employed if we are going to realize the desired results. Again, God can do no more for you than he can do through you.

Emerson holds that the universe comes to us only on its own terms. All the beseeching in the world will not change the nature of reality. Whoever gets in the water will get wet, ice will always feel cold, and fire will always burn. In other words, the elements and laws of nature do not stop us in our prayer and ask, "Do you belong to the church? Are you saved?" For we live in a universe of law!

When we begin to form a consciousness of the presence of God, whose good pleasure it is to give us the Kingdom, we realize that prayer is not conquering God's reluctance. It is synchronizing ourselves in consciousness with the cosmic flow, which is God's eternal willingness.

A person often says, "I asked God for help in this problem, and God said 'No!'" What a distorted and limited understanding of the infinite! God's mind is the great affirmative. There is no negative in God. God never says never! God always says "Yes!" It is we who are the nay-sayers. The more important question is "What do you say?"

God is life, and life is whole. Life can only seek to express and perfect life. So if you pray for life, life can only say "Yes!" What can life know but life? Can light know darkness? Can air know a vacuum? Thus, your prayer, for life or for health, must be your commitment to get into the spirit of life. And your prayer is amiss unless it relates affirmatively with life. Let your prayer say "Yes!" to life: "I am an ever-unfolding expression of perfect life."

We have misunderstood the Bible and Jesus' teachings on this point. In Job we read, "Thou shalt also decree a thing and it shall be established unto thee, and light shall shine upon thy ways" (22:28, ASV). It doesn't shine because we decree it. It shines because the universe is calling, and because the decree is the movement in our consciousness to synchronize the light within, which is eternal. John said, "The true light that enlightens every man was coming into the world" (John 1:9).

Jesus understood this process, and his life was a tribute to its effectiveness. He was not one in whom God specialized, but one who specialized in God. His whole life was conditioned by the truth because of his steady effort to make it so. And we misunderstand him if we think that he didn't have to work with effort and discipline just as we do.

Jesus was forever affirming the truth for himself and others. This fact has been obscured because the early translators had no concept of "affirmative acceptance." Thus, many of his statements and prayers were twisted into petitions and supplications for help. A careful and objective study of the original texts reveals that all Jesus' prayers were affirmations. For instance, the Lord's Prayer, though traditionally set in the tone of supplication, when viewed in the tone of modern translations becomes an affirmative statement, a classic spiritual treatment:

> Our father in heaven, hallowed is your name. Your Kingdom is now coming forth, your will is always being done, in earth as it is in Heaven. You give us this day our daily bread. You always forgive as we forgive. You would never lead us into temptation, but are the very power of deliverance from limitation . . . For yours is the Kingdom, and the power, and the glory, for ever, Amen.

One powerful affirmation!

When people heard Jesus saying, "I am the light of the world," they thought he was referring to himself, that he was announcing that he was God, or God's special agent. But he was simply affirming the truth, or "throwing the switch." And he made it clear that each of us must also affirm the truth.

The true affirmation is: I AM. This was the key to Jesus' power: his affirmation and realization of I AM. Not "I want to be," "I hope to be," "I will be someday," or "Dear Lord, make me to be." But simply: I AM. Recall that occasion in the wilderness when Moses heard the inner voice urging him to undertake the task of leading the Israelites out of their enslavement in Egypt and on to their promised land. Moses was meek and, in his own self-image, "slow of speech." He asked, "But who should I say hath sent me?" And the voice boomed, "You shall say to the people, 'I AM that I AM' hath sent you."

Jesus constantly affirmed this I AM. To understand the esoteric meaning of the Gospels, it is important to know when Jesus is speaking in human consciousness, and when he is speaking in the I AM consciousness. If you have a red-letter edition of the New Testament, you are aware that all Jesus' words appear in red letters. This makes for easy reference. It may be that there should also be a green-letter edition. This would enable us to quickly identify his words spoken in the Christ consciousness. One example would be his Gethsemane experience, where in human consciousness he prayed, "If it be possible, let this cup pass from me"; and then in the Christ consciousness he affirmed, "Nevertheless, not as I will but as thou wilt" (Matt. 26:39). (The universe is calling . . . and now I am listening.)

Among the green words would be:

"I AM the bread of life."
"I AM the light of the world."
"I AM the true vine."
"I AM the good shepherd."
"I AM the door of the sheep."
"I AM the resurrection and the life."
"I AM the way, the truth, and the life."

How did this I AM concept become obscure and lost, giving rise to the confusing concept of the divinity of Jesus? For the most part it was the result of faulty translations. A classic example is John 8:24. Your Bible probably renders this: "If ye believe not that I am he, ye shall die in your sins" (John 8:24, KJV). The word *he* was not in the original manuscript. The first translators could not understand that Jesus was simply affirming the truth: "Except ye believe that I AM . . . " The "I AM" does not need an object. Trying to be helpful, they inserted the *he* of their own volition. In a marginal notation in some Bibles it is indicated that the *he* was added for "clarity." Clarity! In actuality this one faulty translation has had as much responsibility as anything for the failure in Christianity to perceive the true mission of Jesus and the true focus of his teaching.

John 8:24 is actually a powerful realization: "Unless you believe the I AM, you will experience the frustration of the divine flow"—which is what the progressive movement toward deterioration and death really is.

So a vital part of prayer is the "I AM" realization of our good, tuning in on the creative flow, entering the inner chamber and letting God say "Yes" through us.

In the study of truth we become aware of the role of consciousness. We discover that we often slip into a negative attitude, in which we say "No!" to the creative flow of good. Thus prayer becomes a process of letting go of the negative, and affirming the positive, claiming our good, saying "Yes" to life.

We have suggested a three-step formula in prayer: (1) relax and let go of the problem; (2) get grounded in silent communion at the "still point" within; and then (3) project the energy built up in our silent time . . . through an affirmative word.

It is not our intention to stress these steps in any mechanical prayer technique that must be used faithfully in your prayers. It is simply a training framework to help you to get the right perception of the spiritual process. In time, with practice, you may simply close your eyes, go right into a consciousness of oneness, and experience a conviction that "it is finished."

Remember, you pray with your consciousness, not as an escape from it. It is good to take a few moments prior to your prayer experience to reflect on the truth that God loves you. God is a healing flow within you. God is a directing influence that is ever with you . . . constantly, and not just when you are using the right prayer words.

Before you commence your prayer time it is good to do some preparation. You will need to have ready some words of truth or affirmations to use following your experience in the silence. Many persons simply take a prayer out of a prayer book. However, I suggest that you begin to think in terms of creating your own affirmations and treatments. If you are really serious about making a new beginning with the science of prayer, you will be willing to let your words of prayer flow forth out of the same source from which your help will come. Whatever may be the problem, it is *in* you. And recalling our thoughts about the cosmic counterpart, the answer is also in you.

You might be thinking, "But I wouldn't know what to say." Then you should profit greatly from this exercise by which you can formulate affirmations that will be unerringly relevant to your needs.

Take a spiral notebook. Turn to a clean page. Give some thought to the problem areas of your life. What are you worried about? What is "bugging" you? What have you been struggling with in prayer? Make a list of all that you can think of.

Prioritize your list, giving each item a number: 1, 2, 3, etc.—the order in which you want to approach them. Select the "top priority" concern and, turning to a new page, write this concern as a heading. Now divide the page into three columns.

In the first column, write a brief description of the problem: what is wrong—your fears, anxieties, resentments, discouragement. In the second column ask yourself, "How do I think things ought to be?" There is a sense of oughtness within each of us. It comes from the intuitive awareness that there is more in us and more for us. The universe is calling us to accept that more. Sometimes we pervert the oughtness process by taking the rebellious "there-ought-to-be-a-law" stand. This leads to resentment and resistance. It is positive thinking, but you are positively negative. Transpose the "problem paragraph" from your first column into an "oughtness" mode. Where you said, "I am discouraged about my physical condition . . . " you can say, "I ought to be strong and confident in the healing power within." Other sentences in this oughtness paragraph could be transposed, "I ought to be able to rise above pain," "As a child of God, I ought to be free from the influence of contagion." Play with this oughtness transposition. It will expose you to an important side of your nature. And, believe it or not, it will reveal the roots of faith and an innate confidence that there is a way. Now you are halfway home. In your sense of oughtness you are touching that intuitive feeling that is the cosmic counterpart of you. That which ought to be is a present reality. So now, in the third column, transpose the "ought-to-be" paragraph from your second column into a series of I AM statements. "I ought to be healthy" becomes "I am whole." "I ought to be able to rise above physical pain" becomes "Through the power within me I am free from pain and resistance to pain." Transpose all the "ought-to-be's." It may seem awkward at first, but as with all activities, you will gain in confidence and proficiency with practice.

You have created some affirmations that, used together, form a spiritual treatment. The beauty of this is that they came out of your analysis of yourself. They are yours. They are you. You can use them effectively in your prayer time. You can take other problems on your priority list, and, using another clean page in your notebook, you can formulate another set of working affirmations. Work with this exercise. You may surprise yourself with how resourceful you become and how effective your prayer practice will be. And, even more, this notebook may become your own "book of common prayer."

Now you are ready for an effective prayer experience. Begin with the step of relaxation and letting go, physically working with a relaxation drill, letting go of your tensions and strain, and mentally letting go of concerns and anxieties. Have your silence of going into yourself, feeling oneness with cosmic energy. Then . . . turn to the affirmations relative to the particular need you may be working with.

Speak the words, your words. Recall the image of the archer, with arrow in place, and sense the drawing back of the bow, building up the latency of transcendent energy. Then release the arrow. See it going forth to accomplish that whereto it is sent.

Now remember, you do not speak the words to make them true. The truth is true even before you affirm it. So you affirm it, not to get a response from God, but to become synchronized in consciousness, to let the ever-present healing action unfold. You are not praying *to* God *about* your problem. You are getting in tune with the divine process. "The Father knows what you need before you ask Him" (Matt. 6:8) and "It is your Father's good pleasure to give you the Kingdom" (Luke 12:32)—to manifest wholeness, prosperity, and fulfillment.

Sickness is a fact, but it is not the truth. So you affirm the truth to become established in the awareness of the greater potential that is within you. Lack may be an experience, but it is not a spiritual reality. So you affirm the reality. You may have a depleted bank account or an empty wallet, but you can never be cut off from the wealth of the universe. You may affirm, "I am wise with the wisdom of spirit." But this does not suddenly make you wise. It conditions you to experience the wisdom that has been yours since "before the world was." This is why Jesus claimed, "Before Abraham was, I AM" (John 8:58).

Consider a child learning the multiplication tables by rote. Eventually, these formulas are on the tip of his or her consciousness whenever they are needed. But when the child repeats "two times two equals four," this does not make it so. The child repeats it to know that it *is* so, and to align his or her thinking and figuring with the action of this immutable mathematical principle.

Praying for more love, more life, more guidance, more substance, is not a matter of trying to bring more *to* you, but to awaken to the more that has always been you. Paul says, "Stir up the gift of God, which is in thee" (2 Tim. 1:6, KJV). This doesn't mean to stir God to action, but rather to stir up your own awareness that you have been frustrating the flow with your "No!" attitudes . . . and to awaken the commitment to return to a life-affirming "Yes!" consciousness.

When you understand the process of scientific prayer, it seems so very right and natural to affirm for yourself:

> God is my life; I am an expression of God and thus perfect life is my heritage. I accept perfect life as my life. I know that every cell and organ and function of my body temple is animated and renewed by God's perfect life.

This is spiritual treatment!

It is a conditioning flow of life-affirming words. This affirming treatment, however, is not intended for God's ears, telling him that this is what he is supposed to be, and to "get on the job." Rather, the object is to condition your mind and your entire experience with God-consciousness. As we have said, it is not praying *to* God *about* things. It is conditioning your mind with the dynamics of spiritual consciousness, and projecting that consciousness toward that which concerns you.

Let me repeat: you do not pray *to* God, but from a consciousness *of* God. Think about this. Get it into your awareness. So whenever you have something to pray about, before you start looking up and reaching out, pause for a moment and remember: first get the awareness of oneness, as a mighty potential of life, substance, and intelligence within you. Then set about spiritedly to pray from that awareness.

You see, this affirmative prayer approach, the I AM consciousness, saying "Yes" to life and success, should help you to understand the idea of positive thinking. The line is pretty fine between positive thinking and affirmative prayer treatment. Actually, what you think about anything at any time is a treatment of that thing. It is a kind of prayer. In other words, it is important to put into words only those things that you will be happy to see taking shape in your life. For negative thoughts, anxiety and worry, are prayer treatments, and quite effective too. You may be saying, "Oh, I don't like the signs being given off by the economy. I am so fearful that my investments will fail." You have invested your energy in a negative image, and you will get results. Take hold of yourself. "Stir up the gift of God within you." Get yourself on a life-affirming level. It is a critical moment for you. Turn the vibration around, so that you are in tune with the positive flow. A golden rule: "Never let a discussion end on a negative tone. Take care to turn to the 'upbeat.'"

You may have thought that you were only praying when you said, "Now I am going to start praying." No matter what you call it, your thought concerning any subject is a prayer treatment. What is your thought right now about your body? your eyes? your stomach? your heart? You are treating these vital organs with these thoughts. Are you conditioning them with a negative energy? You could say, "I wish I knew what is upsetting my stomach. I am so concerned that it might be something serious." You have answered your own question. You are what is upsetting your stomach. Love your stomach, this great workshop of your body. Bless it. Form the image of your stomach busily processing all the foods you give it like a great complex factory, and passing on to the life stream the substances needed to sustain a strong and vital body.

When you talk about "my weak heart," "my back trouble," or "my asthma," you are actually treating these conditions, making a reality of them. If you keep telling yourself how awful you feel, how insufficient you are, you are saying "No!" to the greatness of the universal creative process trying to be you. Stop thinking how poor, how sick, how inadequate you are. Generate a conditioning flow of spiritual energy by affirming, "I am a wonderful child of God, wondrously created and wonderfully sustained."

Now let's become clear about the practice of affirmation. It is not a verbal attempt to make something happen. Belief that the words you speak are going to accomplish something could give rise to intensity and pressure, even voicing the words with increased emotion. One teacher tells his students to "Speak the word loudly with authority so that God will know that you are serious." If God doesn't know when you are serious, then God doesn't know anything. Actually, "The Father knows even before you ask . . . " Some teachers say we should repeat the affirmation three times over . . . even ten times. But this is to miss the whole point. It is not important how many times you repeat a statement, or how loudly or softly, or if you voice no word at all. The important thing is to get yourself into a "Yes" consciousness, synchronized with the inner flow of God. When you understand this, there will be no pressure, no "vain repetitions," no loud proclamations. Your words will be spoken (even whispered) like a feather on the breeze.

Don't complicate the prayer process by thinking of the affirmations and treatments as mystical and magical words. They are actually the original "let there be" of Genesis. They are very simply the means by which you get in tune with the divine flow. You do not speak the affirmative word to make something happen. The problem in your experience evidences that in some way you have been blocking the flow. Relax! Relax! Be still and know that "I AM." That is all that is needed. Whisper, "I AM life. I AM life."

It is not looking up or straining out to God. The story is told that Emmet Fox once said to a study class, "My friends, you are too tense. If God were up there, as your actions seem to imply, I would have hired the suite above us for our lecture." This is why, before you commence praying or meditating, it is good to rehearse the realization, "God is present as a dynamic presence within me. God is present as a force of love and of life and of intelligence that is in support of me at all times." This is to remind yourself that you are not trying to reach God or to get his attention. Then when you get still, you will easily "go down your well" to a dynamic sense of oneness with the infinite.

We want you to think of praying in terms of action words: affirming and treating. You are a creature of action, thus you will invariably be either worrying or faithing, wholing or sicking, riching or pooring, successing or failing. So you are always treating yourself with some focus of consciousness. In a very real sense you are always "praying without ceasing." Your responsibility is to choose the level of consciousness on which you deal with the everyday experiences of life. You can go on worrying, fearing, engaging in all kinds of negative thinking

. . . or you can engage in scientific prayer. This involves letting go, centering yourself at the "still point" within, in an awareness of oneness with the divine flow, and then speaking the word, affirming the truth in a treatment of positive power.

The all-important realization is that the divine flow is always within you. It is an unborn possibility of limitless life, and yours is the privilege of giving birth to it. The universe is calling. Are you listening? This is what prayer is all about.

CHAPTER 9

The Great Amen

It may seem unusual to devote one whole chapter in a book on prayer to the word *Amen*. What is there to think or talk about? You simply say *Amen* at the conclusion of the prayer, and that's all there is to it. Right? Wrong! *Amen* is one of the most powerful words in our language. Certainly it is a most common word in the lexicon of all Western religions. But it is a word that has been reduced to its perfunctory use in liturgy . . . and its inner meaning has by and large been lost.

There is an interesting line in Shakespeare's *Macbeth*. Macbeth is wallowing in guilt and remorse: "I could not say 'Amen' when they did say 'God bless us.' But wherefore could not I pronounce 'Amen.' I had most need of blessing, and 'Amen' stuck in my throat."[1] And it just could be that the reason why so often our prayer seems to be static and unfulfilled is that, figuratively, 'Amen' sticks in our throats.

Let's take a long look at this mighty mite of a word, *Amen*. In the King James version of the Bible, the "Amen" is interpreted to mean *so be it*. Many teachers and ministers use this "so be it" for "Amen" in public prayer, as more expressive of the correct mood. It is important to note that in the Old English the words *so be it* did not mean *so it will be*, or *in God's good time*. They meant *so it is; it is done; it is finished, now*.

In the ancient Hebrew and Greek in which the Bible was written, the *Amen* normally is given to mean, "Verily . . . it is established . . . it is true . . . this is the Truth."

In the first chapter of Genesis the *Amen* is very much involved in the original form. To understand the book of Genesis, once again we have a lot of unlearning to do as a result of our past religious training. For we have been taught that the first chapter of Genesis deals with God creating the world in seven days. This is the creationist's theme that is so much in the news in the ongoing feud with the evolutionists. In this scenario God created Adam out of mud, then he created Eve out of Adam's rib, then she gave birth to Cain and Abel, and after Cain slew Abel, Eve gave birth to Seth. Then Seth went off into the Land of Nod and there he married and had children. Few of the creationists have noticed how this shows a serious flaw in the literal acceptance of the creation story. For if they went off into another country and married, where did the women come from, since it had all just commenced in Eden?

It is questionable whether the Genesis story has anything to do with the creation of the world in a literal time frame. It was written during the captivity of the Israelites in Babylon. It was written by Jewish prophets who were sensing that the Israelites were losing their Jewish identity, their culture, their unique awareness of God. So, in an attempt to bring the people back to a sense of pride in their identity as Jews, they went back and rewrote all the myths and allegories that had come down in their culture, putting them together in a form designed to elicit new faith and new patriotism. This is when the Genesis story was written. It was not a history of the creation. It was never intended to be anything other than symbolic.

In the first chapter of Genesis, after each day (which symbolically portrayed a step in the universal creative process), it says, "And God said, 'Let there be light'; and there was light." Or "God said, 'Let there be a firmament' . . . and it was so." In the original Hebrew, this statement, "It was so," was written "Amen." So originally it would have read, "And God said, 'Let us make man in our image, after our likeness; and let them have dominion over . . . all the earth. . . . Amen.' " This is the original *Amen*. A lot of *Amens* of the Bible have been penciled out by translators simply because they didn't think they made very much sense.

In the second chapter of Genesis, we are told that God caused every living thing to pass before Adam, and whatever he called it, that became its name. Now remember, the creation story is an allegory dealing with the divine creative process, both universally and personally. "The Lord God" here is divine law. God wasn't looking for names for his creatures. It had nothing to do with what the creature was. But it had everything to do with what it became as far as Adam was concerned. This evidences the law of consciousness. Things always become to us what we see them as being. For instance, a child is drawing a picture. His teacher says, "And what is that supposed to be, Johnny?" The lad proudly says, "It is a tree." True, his was a scraggly looking tree, but still that is the way he perceived it. The unwise teacher says, "That's not what a tree is supposed to look like. Here, let me show you . . . Now that's what a tree is supposed to look like." The unfoldment of his creative ability receives a terrible blow at this moment, a shock from which he may never recover. The child drew a tree as he saw it. The teacher drew a tree as she saw it. What a tree really is may be something entirely different from either of them.

Again, it is an indication of the law of consciousness. What we believe about a thing affects what it becomes to us. Obviously, we are saying *Amen* to things all the time.

In the New Testament, *Amen* is used as an adverb, to mean *yea, truly, verily, for a certainty*. The earliest manuscript of the Gospel quotes Jesus as saying, "Amen, Amen, I say unto you . . . " But in later translations, as you will note in your Bible, it now reads, "Verily, verily, I say unto you." But the *Amen* had a deeper significance. "This is the Truth. . . . This is the Truth. I say unto you."

Now in the course of time it became customary to use *Amen* only at the close of public songs, prayers, and benedictions. It has become a kind of ecclesiastical punctuation mark, to be uttered at the close of the worship service, perhaps sung chorally, "Amen, Amen," or at the end of a prayer, such as the Lord's Prayer. Thus, in effect, all the mystical implication has been lost for the average person.

It is interesting to note that the ancient Egyptians, centuries before the time of Jesus, realized the power of *Amen*. You find it incorporated into the names of the great leaders, such as Pharaoh Amenhotep, Tutankhamen, Amen-Ra, to name just a few. To the Egyptians *Amen* meant *master* or *ruler*. Again, this is a fundamental realization of truth. It is an important clue to the science of prayer. Whatever you unite your *Amen* to becomes your master and rules you.

You may be talking about the fact that there is a new strain of flu virus "going around." You blurt out, "I sure hope I don't get it." And you have to that degree become established in a fear consciousness. You are saying *Amen* to the possibility of coming down with it. Not that this means you will get it, but it establishes your vulnerability. Remember, whatever you unite your *Amen* to becomes your master and rules you. As soon as you unite any thought with your *Amen*, with feeling, you give it the full power of your mental acceptance. That thought becomes your master or ruler, and that thought will be made manifest in your conscious world.

Now when we catch the implication of *Amen*, we can see the error of traditional prayer, i.e., "O God I am sick and troubled. Help me. Amen." What this says is that your sickness and troubles are what you are really believing in. You are saying *Amen* to limitation. You are saying, "This is the Truth. I accept it." Do you really accept it? Do you also accept the fact that you are a "miserable sinner?"

I once attended a small denominationally endowed college in the Midwest. I was doing graduate work in music at a fine conservatory of this school. There was a chapel service every day, with required attendance. The seminary attached to the college provided the student ministers to lead the worship service. It was obvious that they were vying with one another as to how much fire and brimstone they could get into their sermons. Every day the words *miserable sinner* were used dozens of times. And I have thought, whimsically, when the students in attendance were constantly saying *Amen* to it, that it may be a small miracle that many of the students did not turn out to be delinquents.

Traditionally, prayer has been a time of pouring out all one's troubles, counting them over, one by one, in the delusion and voiced hope that God would have mercy. But God cannot have mercy on you, for there is no "un-mercy" in God. God cannot forgive you, for there is no unforgiveness in divine mind. The unforgiveness is in you. You have to let it go. Jesus said, "The Father knows what things you have need of even before you ask him."

So don't use your prayer time to ask God a lot of irrelevant questions. "The Father knows . . . and it is his good pleasure to give you the Kingdom." Your need is to let go, and open yourself to the divine flow. You need not outline problems. For the danger is that, in outlining them, you deify them and then say *Amen* to them. The true impact of your prayer is the stamp, "This is the truth," that you put on them. So we should never voice any prayer on which we are not willing to put the stamp of *Amen*.

So, you see, *Amen* is much more than a word. It is a peculiar force of consciousness. Any time you accept something as true, you are saying *Amen* to it. And you can be sure that if there is some difficulty in your life, in some way, at some time you have said *Amen* to it—perhaps not in so many words, but in the state of consciousness that the words imply.

It is a fundamental truth that you will never experience anything in the world of your body and affairs that you have not previously accepted in one form or another into your mind and heart. This is what I call *the law of acceptance*. And this is the implication of the "Great Amen."

We talk a lot about consciousness. But consciousness is your own. There is a great freedom of choice involved. Your reaction to a person depends completely on what you are identifying with, which also says much about you. A person may be good and kind and lovable, but have a habit that is annoying to you. So you say *Amen* to that, and it is possible to let it become that person's whole character in your feeling about the person. You may say, "She is just that kind of person." This is what prejudice is all about. She is not "that kind of person." She, or he, is a person who may actually be loving, and faithful, and courageous, and truthful, but who happens to have a little idiosyncrasy or minor weakness. Who's perfect?

Say *Amen* to the good of a person's nature, and suddenly the whole relationship will begin to change for the good. Of course the real change is in you, not necessarily in him or her. Pray for her, bless him, behold the Christ in them. Now you are saying *Amen* to the good in that person. Bless the person every time he or she walks into your space, and the thing that annoys you will probably stop.

However, if you have a prejudiced view of the person, whenever you are together, your consciousness will almost insist that the annoying thing that distresses you so much must happen. You may even be disturbed if it doesn't. You may be thinking. "OK, this person is acting nice now, but there is something fishy. They're angling for something."

The question is, what are you saying *Amen* to? When you catch the evening news, there is a panoply of negation, a lot of potential good or evil looking for a place to land. Are you going to accept it? The news of the day, the behavior of people around you, the changes in the economy that affect you, and the vibrations in your home are much like the animals filing before Adam and Eve to be named. You may say of something in the news, "That's terrible . . . simply awful . . . those beasts!" Or you can say, "Bless it. Divine order is established. Only good can come into my life." Which shall it be? You always have a choice.

You can always say with the Psalmist, "I will lift up mine eyes unto the hills, from whence cometh my help" (Ps. 121:1, KJV). And remember, the universe is calling you to "release your imprisoned splendor," to let your light shine.

This is not being an escapist or a Pollyanna. It is not being naive and deluding yourself. It is a matter of synchronizing yourself with a positive energy flowing within you. "Let something good be said!"

We might consider a common situation: a job layoff, or an enforced retirement. You may be understandably shocked and ill-prepared. There is the matter of financial insecurity, the problem of getting another job "at my age." But the greatest shock is the feeling of rejection. "How could they do this to me?"

Make a list of all the negatives you feel about the situation: the hurt, the fears, society's prejudices, everything you can think of that is mentally unhealthy about this experience. Then, when you have completed the list . . . tear it up or burn it. Now make another list of all the positives you can think of about it. It is an opportunity to make a healthy change. It will enable you to reappraise your life, perhaps to get into a different field. Then take an imaginary *Amen* rubber stamp (better yet, have one made), and joyously stamp *Amen* on all the positives. It will give you the reassuring sense of doing something about the problem . . . and make no mistake about it, you are doing something vital.

When you say *Amen* to that which is good, you put the full weight of your mental and spiritual acceptance on it . . . and you make contact with the force that will work to bring it to pass. As an example, when I was a child, it was common practice for mothers to tell their youngsters, "Now don't get your feet wet or you will catch your death of cold." I am sure you could make a long list of such clichés that have had a profound influence on you. You may have said *Amen* to the "wet-feet-cold" syndrome for so long that you have rarely questioned it, so for years colds have come from wet feet, almost as if you absorbed the germs through the soles of your feet.

Many young men served in the military in World War II. As a training officer in the Army Medical Corps, it was my job, through orientation and training films, to present the facts relative to the "death-of-cold-wet-feet" syndrome: that it was simply not true, that no person ever got a cold from wet feet (or out of a draft). These soldiers often lived in water and mud conditions for weeks on end and rarely had a cold. What they had done was to begin saying *Amen* to something entirely different, the potential of the body to sustain itself in wellness.

When you hear a discouraging medical prognosis, do you accept it in resignation? If you do, you make a god out of the doctor, who is only telling you what he sees (a puddle and wet feet). He is dealing with the life-force in you on a purely physical level. But, if you listen, "the universe is calling," a life force which the doctor himself calls the *vic-medicatrix naturae* (the healing power of nature). Let the call of the universe whisper in your ear, "You are a spiritual being, and there is a force within you that transcends the facts of the case, and the possibility of remission and healing is always present."

In 2 Corinthians 1:20 Paul says, "For all the promises of God find their Yes in him. That is why we utter the Amen through him, to the glory of God." This is an important insight in the practice of truth. We must be constantly on the alert in what we accept as being true for us. There are always rumor-mongers, crepe-hangers, and pessimists, who point with alarm. There is always a book that fear has made a bestseller, predicting a great depression in the near future. You see, it doesn't make good sense to live your life from the outside, to let news reports, forecasts, and people determine how you are going to think, feel, and live.

Unemployment is the tragic experience of many persons. If you should be laid off in an industry cutback, or forced into an early retirement for which you are financially unprepared, remember, you may be fired from a job, but there is no way that you can be fired from the universe—unless you accept the idea of separation. One of the problems of unemployment, however it may come about, is the feeling of being unneeded, put out to pasture. You must say "No!" to this feeling, and affirm that you are a vital part of the creative flow of the universe. You are one with God, and nothing can keep you out of the creative flow of ideas, and of love and fulfillment. Nothing . . . but you.

There is another meaning of the statement, "By his hand we are given 'Amen' to the glory of God." Always be sure to put a period at the end of any prayer. Never leave your prayer effort up in the air with a question mark. If you pray as you may have done in the past, a kind of perfunctory prayer of supplication, there may be a sense of "Well, I prayed. I hope God heard me." Thus, there is a subtle question mark at the end. It is not a matter of "Did God hear you?" More importantly, are you hearing God and his ceaseless longing to express himself more fully in you? The universe is calling: listen . . . listen . . . and accept. Speak the word of truth, and then *Amen, it is done, so be it.*

We have previously noted that affirmations and metaphysical treatments have little power of themselves. There is no magic in the words we use. The "magic" is in the believing consciousness with which we articulate the words. If the perception is clear enough there is a point where "the word which you hear is not mine but the Father's who sent me" (John 14:24). Your affirmation may be, "I am strong and whole now." This statement could potentially be a pipeline to the divine healing flow. But if it is made in the consciousness of "I sure hope it works," then you are believing in the problem more than the solution. You are saying *Amen* to your fears. You are in tune with the indefinite, practicing the "absence" of God. However, if you are centered in the divine flow, your affirmation gives focus to a greater healing power, in which you can say as a statement of accomplished fact, "I am strong and whole now."

Say *Amen* to your good. Put the stamp of acceptance on that which you want to see manifest. And when you pray or treat, be sure that the words are ones to which you want to give total acceptance, and say *Amen* to that.

Dear reader, hear me with your heart when I remind you,

the universe is calling, singing its song of life and love into your whole being. You are one with the divine flow. You are in tune with health and substance and love and peace. You walk and work in tune with the infinite process that turns all things of your life to good . . . and to this I say *Amen!*

CHAPTER 10

How to Pray for Others

You may wonder, when we talk about eliminating so much of the ritual of prayer, what about the beautiful prayers of tradition? What about the Twenty-third Psalm, the Ninety-first Psalm, the Lord's Prayer? Such works, beautiful as they are, have no special credit with God. They are poems, quiet reveries, spiritual musings that may lift your spirits. But they are important only to the degree that they do uplift us. If they become a ritual and we say them perfunctorily, then they lose any spiritual power whatever.

Now, even as background music may help to set the vibration in which you do good work, so reading some of these musings may set a good tone in consciousness for a prayer experience. For instance, you may voice the Lord's Prayer as a part of your prayer time, but when you speak the words, it is important to know what they mean, and mean what they imply when you say them.

No words of prayer, not even the lovely Jewish Shema ("Hear, O Israel, the Lord God is one"), have any special reception in the heart of God. Yet if you can get the realization of oneness that the words imply, you may become synchronized with a flow of divine power.

The psalmist heard the universe calling, and he listened, and the words of the Twenty-third Psalm flowed forth through him. You may hear the universe calling as you read the words of the psalm. and in the same way you will open the intuitive flow in you, unfolding as your own song of life.

Now, you may be thinking, "Okay, this emphasis on oneness in prayer is good. I am not to pray to God for help, but to know my oneness, and to pray from that consciousness. But how do I pray for others? Can I change their life by changing my thoughts?"

Perhaps you should ask yourself, "Why do I want to change another person?" It is a great waste of human energy . . . this frustrated desire or effort to change other people: to help a loved one to overcome a weakness or heal an illness, or resolve conflicts, to make antagonists cease antagonizing. Changing other people may well be meddling in their affairs. I said it is a waste of energy to try to change another, not because people can't change, but because change is a growth process from within the person's own self.

More often than not, the desire to change other people is the desire to make them into something they are not. But the plain truth is, they can never be other than what they are. Of course what they are is good enough, if they can just stop frustrating their potential. They need only to be themselves, just more so than ever before.

You may say, "But shouldn't we try to help people who are hurting? Isn't it natural for a good person to be concerned?" Of course it is natural. It is also natural for your finger to burn when it touches a hot stove. But you would respond reflexively and pull your finger away before there was a burn. When you are concerned about one who is ill or who is facing a crisis, you may suffer with that person vicariously. You hurt too. You may say, "My heart bleeds for you." Thus, you may tend to respond sympathetically to the person in crisis or in pain. It is very human to have a concern, but it is not wise to act impulsively on the concern in human consciousness. As long as an impulsive concern leads the way in prayer, you will fail to achieve positive results.

The important need is not to try to effect some change in other people, but to make some changes in your thoughts about them. Don't try to set them right, but rather to see them rightly. And to see them rightly you must get rid of some narrow frames of reference, and get out of the feeling of concern. This is not to say it is easy, but to establish that it is possible.

There is a divine mind milieu in which you live and move and have being . . . and the same is true for the one about whom you are concerned. This is why thoughts of love or protection tend to evoke a subtle response in the other person. When you love another person, something in that person feels it and responds to it in some way. And when you think about the person you love, there is a response in that person to your thought. Research has revealed that plants in a room show a measurable response on an EKG to strong thoughts and emotions about them. Praise and love them, and they tend to flourish. Curse or criticize them, and they may be stunted. If it is true of plants, it seems more than likely that it is also true of people.

Thus, when you worry about a loved one—the child on the way home from school, the wayward youth who has run off to some commune, the husband with the alcohol problem, the friend in the hospital—you are putting the full weight of your consciousness on the side of their difficulty. You are hindering their progress . . . you actually become a part of their problem.

When you want to help someone about whom you are concerned, the important work is to be done in you. As far as you are concerned, the problems out there, no matter what or whom they involve, exist in your mind, your prejudices, your fears, and your anxious concern. So your work, initially, is to change your thoughts, to heal and resolve your concern.

This is why it is so very difficult to pray for one you love: your child, your spouse, a very close friend. You may defend your anxious concern by saying, "But you don't understand, it's my baby!" But I do understand, I have been there. You must make a choice: do you want to help your baby (or another person), or do you insist on standing in their way? You must heal your concern. You must let go and release your loved one into God's care and keeping. The work to be done is in you, on your consciousness, not in the other person. You must change your thoughts. You may object, "But it is her thought that is negative!" But it is your thought that is disturbed about it, and that personal disturbance is negative. There is no way that you can reach into another person's mind and erase all negative thoughts, despite your great love for them. You can only radiate what I call "the contagion of a triumphant spirit" that comes when you clear your own mind, and get yourself centered and in tune. If you don't alter your thoughts, but remain upset and concerned about this other person, then you will be a part of their problem.

A man was distraught over his young son who was into drugs and alcohol. He was angry and insulted by the suggestion of a counselor that he was part of his son's problem. But, eager to find the truth, in time he did, in fact, accept some responsibility for what was happening in his son, realizing that as long as his thoughts about the son were focused on worry and parental concern, he was giving support to the weakness. He had to learn to "let go and let God," and it wasn't easy. In such cases we hold on desperately. We don't want to let go. But if we really want to help, there is no other way.

This father worked diligently to alter his anxious concern, and then he prayed, not to God about his son, but from the consciousness of God, projecting this consciousness to the son, saluting the divinity in him, seeing him strong and whole. Of course he realizes that this alone will not do the work for the son. The answer can only come from within the young man himself. But the father made a great effort to overcome his own attitudes and responses. There is no way to know how or even why such results occur, but it is more than coincidence that the young man is well on the road to recovery.

When I say "I have been there," I really mean it. When my oldest son was about five years old, he rode his tricycle down a long flight of stone steps, sustaining a huge swelling on his forehead where his head struck the concrete sidewalk. I rushed him to the emergency room of a nearby hospital. Of course, my boy was screaming in pain. The doctor was having a difficult time holding him still in order to treat him. And, need I add, I was hurting with him. I suddenly became aware of the fact that I was adding to the problem in my understandably sympathetic parental reaction. So I walked out of the room, down the hall, out of the hospital, and down the driveway to the road. Here I sat on the curb with my head in my hands, wisely taking charge of myself. I knew I had to let go and block the experience out of my mind. It was not easy, for thoughts of "But this is my son" kept clamoring for attention. In time I succeeded in getting quiet, and eventually felt a beautiful sense of peace, life, and wholeness. Presently I realized with a start where I was and what I was facing. I thought of the young boy in the receiving room, but now without anxiety. As I returned to the hospital and on into the emergency room, I felt good about it. I knew all was well. I found the boy sitting up in a chair smiling. The doctor had drained the swelling and put a bandage on the bruise. He said, "A few minutes after you left the room, the boy became quiet and relaxed. It was amazing!" It was startlingly evident that I had been part of the problem. But, you see, I wasn't praying for the boy out there on the curb. I was letting go, knowing peace. And because of the strong love bond between us, he was effectively blessed by my peaceful thoughts.

When Jesus stood before the tomb of his friend Lazarus, he didn't cry out, "Dear Lord, this is my friend, please help him." If that had been the state of his consciousness, there would have been no dramatic resurrection. The account says, "He lifted up his eyes and gave thanks." He was not looking off into the skies for help "from above." He turned his thoughts away from the grim appearance that surely would have spelled grief and hopelessness . . . and turned to the truth that the "universe was calling." And by giving thanks, he gave way to the mystic life flow. From his mind was erased the fact of a body three days in the tomb, and also his personal feelings of loss. His mind was open and receptive to the universe calling . . . "I am the resurrection and the life." And as he continued to listen, the words came forth from his lips, "Lazarus, come forth." And Lazarus walked out of the tomb.

How can we understand such an "impossible" occurrence? I say, don't get caught up in specifics and thus miss the demonstration of the spiritual process. So that we might understand this process in a more general way, let's think about it in the case of your child running to you with a headache or a bruised knee. Because you love the child, you are of course anxiously concerned. But if you really want to help the child, you will quickly "lift up your eyes . . . and give thanks," which means you turn from the appearance, and from your unnerving sympathetic response. You will free the child to its inner healing life, and quietly know that "the universe is calling"; and, listening, let the universe put words into your mouth: "I am perfect healing life." Then, you may speak soothingly and encouragingly to your child. "You are all right. God is your help in every need." By this time the child has stopped crying and says, "You always fix it!" Yes, Mommy always fixes it, Daddy always makes it better, if Mommy and Daddy can first of all heal their anxious concern, listen to the universe calling, and in consciousness become instruments of cosmic healing power.

The reason it is so difficult to pray for the ones you love when they are hurting physically or emotionally is precisely that you love them. You are sympathetically attuned to them. Even as you feel joy with their laughter, you hurt with their pain and discouragement. A father holding his birthing wife's hand may actually have sympathetic "labor pains." Or spouses may feel sad watching each other stoically cover up their obvious disappointment over a setback in business or a crisis in their careers. To really help the other person in this situation is not easy, even for a good student of truth. But always remember that the first, and sometimes only, need is to heal your concern. That means changing your thoughts about the person.

Try to go apart in some way, and get yourself centered, and when you feel at peace about it, you are ready to pray. But be careful to avoid the trap of praying to God for help. Rather, pray from the consciousness of God.

You may be sitting by a friend or loved one in the hospital when the doctor gives a grave prognosis. You may find yourself emotionally swept up in the situation. Instead of sitting there commiserating with a long face, trying hard to look pleasant but feeling terribly sad and worried, it is much better to assure the patient of your love and support, and then leave the room. You will be far more effective having your prayer time in the visitors' waiting room, or out in your car, or when you return home. Don't pray for the "patient in pain" who is back there in the hospital. Rather, get the feeling that the universe is calling, and as you listen you are lifted up to a high awareness of life and wholeness. As you lift yourself, so are you influential in lifting the patient also. For love knows no separation. As Jesus said, "I, if I be lifted up from the earth, will draw all men unto me" (John 12:32, KJV). There is no way to explain logically how it works, but it does work. And you haven't even specifically prayed for the person in words.

Of course, if you want to (and you probably will want to, because it may give you a greater assurance that you are doing something), you may whisper an affirmation of truth or a spiritual treatment for the person. But remember, you are not doing it to make it true, or to make something happen, but only to identify with wholeness, and to see the loved one in this awareness.

The key is "letting go." Unless you can let go, you can't pray effectively for another person. An insistent concern for the other person indicates an unwillingness to let go. You may say, "But you don't understand, it is my mother who is ill, and I am concerned about her. You see, I love her very much." Of course, but if you really love her, you will let go and free her to her own wholeness. Unless you can let go of your concern, and get yourself centered, you will not only be unable to help her, you may actually be hindering her progress, despite your frantic prayers.

Here is a metaphor that has been personally helpful to me. Visualize being in a rowboat by a dock on which the person you want to pray for is standing. Imagine that your prayer is an experience of rowing away from the dock. You may recall that you row a boat facing backwards as you row forwards. Thus, as you row, you face that from which you are rowing. If you are praying effectively, you are moving progressively away from the dock, from the person you are concerned about. As you row, the person keeps getting smaller, until finally they disappear. You have succeeded in getting the person out of the forefront of your consciousness. You have really let go. Oh, the person is still back there on the dock . . . or in the hospital. But you don't have your clutches on them. You free them to their own unfoldment . . . and because you love them, you may be a positive influence in their healing.

How often should you pray for the other person? As often as you find your anxious thoughts creeping back. It is a matter of "change your thoughts and keep them changed." If you find yourself taking responsibility and feeling guilty, feeling that you should be praying more often, then you are "praying amiss."

Someone once asked me, "How can you possibly hold all the people in prayer whom you are praying for?" This supposes that one in my position spends hours at a time holding prayer thoughts about all the persons and situations who have requested such help. I might ask, Do you want me to worry about you all the time, or do you want me to pray for you? If I pray for you, I will "row away" until I can let you go in faith, and free you to your complete healing. Then I may speak a word of truth for you and go on to other things. I am still holding you in a spiritual awareness, but without conscious concern. And if I have a recurring feeling of concern, I go through the letting-go process again.

One person said to me, "I spend all my time praying for my loved ones, and I love it; but it is exhausting." But the truth is, if you are exhausted by prayer, the ego is involved, and you are praying in human consciousness. There is no way that you can be drained by any spiritual effort, if you know that "It is not I, but the Father . . . " Actually, if you are praying aright, in the process of letting the healing power flow through you, you are infilling yourself. If you are working in prayer for a dozen people in a day, you should be that many times stronger at the close of the day. True prayer is not exhausting, ever. Many "healers" would do well to confront themselves with this test of their spiritual integrity.

You may be unaware that you are working in an ego-centered way. Some people give themselves away unwittingly. They may say, "This is what I am doing for these people." And some may say, "I healed that person." Such an attitude is dangerous to the praying person, for they are working at the expense of their inner power, rather than at its expanse.

One thing to keep in mind, when you are praying for a loved one—spouse, child, or close friend—is "Keep the high watch." Keep your loved one in the awareness of wholeness.

Someone may ask, "How is your husband?" Don't fall into a negative state: "Oh, he is having a terrible time. I am praying, but I don't know . . . It is not easy." Instead you can say, "He is going through an experience, but he is doing well. Join us in knowing the truth for him." That's it! Above all, don't get into an "organ recital," sharing information about the condition and a doctor's prognosis. If you discuss the problem in a negative way, then your prayers are counteracted, and you are part of the patient's problem.

What if the one you are praying for is in a distant place? What about "absent treatment?" Remember, the whole of God is present at every point in time and space. So give no thought to distance. I don't like the term "absent treatment." For it implies that you are doing something special, a kind of spiritual voodoo. In truth the presence is present, here and everywhere. So don't get into the thought of distance. Actually, being removed from close proximity with the one who is hurting may be an advantage, for you may not be so tempted to react emotionally to the appearances. If the consciousness is high enough, you should be able to pray for one on the other side of the world as effectively as one on the other side of the room, perhaps even more effectively.

Always remember, the first step in praying for one you want to help is to heal your concern. Let go and "Let God be God in you" . . . and in that other one too.

CHAPTER 11

A Word about Jesus

At this point you may be thinking, "I find myself strongly attracted to your 'New Insight in Truth,' and by this concept of the science of prayer. But one thing troubles me . . . Where does Jesus come in?" My answer to that is, "Jesus never went out." Jesus has been a great influence on my consciousness, and basically, this insight of prayer that we are outlining comes directly from the spirit of his teachings and the works of prayer-dynamics that he demonstrated. Thus, in the interest of getting a clear perception of the prayer process, and so that your mind will be free of doubts and reservations . . . let's take a look at this, my beloved elder brother, Jesus.

Right at the outset we have a problem. It is difficult to approach the subject of Jesus without coming smack up against his name that has been deified, his words that have been codified, and pictures of him that are haloed and unreachable.

I was raised as a Christian in a very conservative Protestant church. Even as a youngster of nine or ten I wanted to know more about Jesus. The Christ on the crucifix, or in the stained glass windows, was completely unreal to me. And my faith was not enhanced when, as an altar boy, I once curiously looked behind the altar and found not a mystic "holy of holies" but simply a storage area cluttered with old candles and used hymnals.

So I should say that I have always been something of an iconoclast. But I have perceived Jesus as one too, which is why he so disturbed the establishment of his day. I must say that I have a deep-seated love for the man, Jesus. For more than fifty years I have been on a personal quest to know what he was about. For, much as I am committed to the absolutes of meta-physical truth, I feel a strong need of the loving compassion engendered by Jesus.

How do you study the life and consciousness of Jesus? You might say, "Through the 'Good Book.'" But that is an oversim-plification. There is an ever-evolving body of knowledge about the Gospels and the milieu in which they were formed. It is now known that the Gospels were written from four different perspectives, and at four different times. During the intervening years before the time they were written down, an oral tradition of the happenings evolved with the inevitable result of glorify-ing the figure of Jesus. What emerged in the Gospel account is a virgin-born, God-ordained, miracle-working, divine creature, beyond any possible human frame of reference.

It has long been my view, which I have espoused in my teaching work for half a century, that Christianity, or perhaps we should say "churchianity," has so emasculated Jesus as to make him totally beyond reach. Too much attention has been given to Jesus' divinity, and not enough to his humanity. Not to question his divinity, but I want to make clear that every person is essentially divine, and that Jesus was the one who discovered the divine depth as a potential within all persons. And he demonstrated the full potential in manifest form.

It is a shock to some persons, reared in a tradition that refers to Jesus as "very God," to consider that he was a man, "In every respect . . . yet without sinning" (Heb. 4:15). He ate and drank and had friends and enemies. He laughed and cried. He was criticized for going to parties and associating with what we might call "the beautiful people." He slept much outdoors, was extremely dark of skin, and never ate with a fork in his life.

Here is a significant comment about Jesus by Charles Fillmore, co-founder of the Unity Movement:

He was more than any other person who ever lived on earth . . . because there came into his humanhood a factor to which most persons are strangers. This factor was the Christ consciousness. The unfoldment of this consciousness by Jesus made him God incarnate, because Christ is the mind of God individualized. We cannot separate Jesus Christ from God or tell where the person leaves off and God begins in him. To say we are human persons as Jesus was a human person is not exactly true, because he had dropped that personal consciousness by which we separate ourselves from our true God-self. He became consciously one with the absolute principle of being. He proved in his resurrection and ascension that he had no consciousness separate from that of being, therefore he was this being to all intent and purpose. Yet he attained no more than what is expected of every one of us.[1]

Read Fillmore's last sentence again, "Yet he attained no more than what is expected of every one of us." I am often asked, even after an inspirational lecture, "All this is fine, but do you accept Christ?" By this they mean, "Do you accept Jesus as the 'only begotten son'?" Of course I accept Christ. But that is akin to accepting gravity. There is a principle involved. Christ is the principle of divine sonship, it is "what is expected of every one of us." The Christ of you is that divine potential of you, and the universe calls you to work diligently to release your "imprisoned splendor." This is what life is all about.

As for the "only begotten son," Meister Eckhart brings clarity to the oft-quoted John 3:16 by transposing this phrase to "that which is begotten only of God." There was that of Jesus that was begotten only of God, the Christ of him. But he taught and his life proved that *every* person has that inner quality which is begotten only of God. The trouble is that in human consciousness there is that which is begotten of Madison Avenue, of the pressures of keeping abreast of styles and fads, and of the race beliefs of poverty, sickness, and war.

It is vitally important that we make a clear distinction between Jesus and the Christ, or else we will fail to grasp the full

significance of the Gospels, and we will miss the point that
Jesus was trying to make. Once I gave a lecture on this subject,
and afterwards a woman said to me, "And to think that for all
my life I have thought that Jesus was the son of Mr. and Mrs.
Christ." It is hilarious, yet it is sad, for it reflects the concept
held by most Christians. The Christ is not Jesus. It is that
which Jesus discovered in himself. But it was the discovery of
the principle of divine sonship that was applicable to all persons. A revealing perspective is to refer to Jesus' Christ, Eric's
Christ, John's Christ, Mary's Christ. Can you understand now?

"But," a questioner asks, "aren't you interested in your salvation?" Of course I am, but salvation is a personal experience.
It calls for taking charge of our life, and progressively releasing
our own God-potential. Jesus didn't come to save the world *en
masse*, but to teach people, one by one, how to find the Christ
indwelling and to walk by its light. So, Jesus is not our re-
deemer. He is the supreme revealer of the truth of our divine
sonship. Our redemption is achieved through changing our own
self-image from pauper to prince, from sinners to masters.

Professor Oliver Reiser, physicist-philosopher at the Univer-
sity of Pittsburgh, writes:

In the long course of social evolution man has sanctified
many things as the source of ultimate power, the object of
veneration and worship. . . . But he has seldom touched
upon man's essential divinity. Never have societies deified
the creative force, the divinity in man. . . . Yet if there is

one thing the Christian mystery sought to teach, it was the divinity within man, the "Christ in you," undeveloped and unheeded.[2]

"Where does Jesus come into our study of prayer?" The whole insight of the inward-out prayer process that this book is articulating has its roots in Jesus' teachings.

The idea that "the universe is calling," the theme of this book, was a very important part of Jesus' life and teachings. But we must note that Jesus uses the word *Father* to mean the energy, the activity, and creative intention of the Universe. "The Son can do nothing of his own accord, but only what he sees the Father doing; for whatever he does, that the Son does likewise" (John 5:19). "The word which you hear is not mine but the Father's who sent me" (John 14:24).

Jesus was a great listener. He heard the universe calling, often. And he dedicated himself to being an instrument by which the universe would call out its message of truth and transformation.

The dynamics, the love, and the light of the Christ flowing forth as words, through Jesus, are actually what this book is about. Jesus set the inward-out tone of prayer when he said, "When thou prayest, enter into thine inner chamber, and having shut thy door, pray to thy Father who is in secret, and thy Father shall reward thee openly" (Matt. 6:6, ASV).

It could hardly be clearer: in prayer, go within to the "still point" of your oneness with God, and in a time of silence, listen, for the universe is calling. In the secret awareness that the whole universe is present where you are, project the life and energy and substance as you pray from this consciousness . . . and the universe will rush and pour and stream into you in fulfillment of your dreams.

CHAPTER 12

Worship and the Power of Group Prayer

In a small town in southern France, I was awakened early one morning by the compelling sound of cathedral bells. I had spent the night in a quaint hotel, a stop-over on my motor tour of France. I looked out the window and observed scores of people silently walking along a winding lane toward the cathedral, undoubtedly to attend morning mass. Inspired by this evidence of devoutness, I quickly dressed and joined the pious pilgrims as we made our way to the cathedral. It was a memorable experience: not so much the celebration of the mass as just the sight of this large group of working people starting their workday with such deep commitment to the worship of their God.

No matter what I may say iconoclastically about formal religion, I am deeply moved by the devoutness of the faithful. And yet, I always feel just a little sad, for it seems to me that so many people are reaching, searching, yearning for an experience of God that can only be found within themselves. The universe is calling, but they can only hear the cathedral bells calling them to come to worship.

The universe is calling us to awaken to oneness. The weary pilgrim journeys forth to church, to shrines, or to the meccas of the world, in search of God. But you do not have to go to church or to any sacred place to get close to God. There is nowhere in all the world where you can get any closer to God than right where you are. God is present in his entirety within you as much as in a great mystic . . . even Jesus. No one can be any closer to God than you, though they may be more aware of their oneness.

Most persons think of prayer as just part of the experience of worship in church on the sabbath. In the Judeo-Christian tradition, the fourth commandment established the institution of sabbath day worship: "Remember the sabbath day to keep it holy. Six days shalt thou labor, but the seventh day is a sabbath to the Lord your God . . . In it you shall not do any work" (Exod. 20:8, 9).

In the early Hebrew culture, keeping the sabbath was mandatory, and in their theocratic society, failure to comply with this commandment to the letter was a capital offense. Numbers, chapter 15, cites the case of a man caught gathering sticks on the sabbath, and he was taken outside the city and stoned to death . . . "as the Lord commanded." An interesting commentary on the prevailing God-concept.

To understand the "how" of prayer, it is important to know how some of the traditional rigid practices have come about.

Today there is a professed concern about what Harvey Cox called "the secular society." But it was institutional religion that created the divisions of "sacred" and "secular," or "holy days" and weekdays. The church has become a place set apart, conducted by a clergy who are a class set apart, on a sabbath which is a day set apart. And all of this is a gross misunderstanding of the wholeness of the universe, a total misreading of the universe calling.

A modern religious commentator has said that the Christian is the least intelligent of all the great types of our race, because the typical Christian has taken the most profound and simple and workable formula ever presented to humanity, and has made of it an umbrella for a rainy day, a nostrum for sickness, and a kind of soul-insurance against disaster.

Sabbath worship is curiously intermingled with the tradition of the "day of atonement," which goes back into the early customs of primitive creatures. They tried to wash away their sins, and to make appeasement to the gods, usually with a blood sacrifice which as we have seen in early cultures was the sacrifice of human life. In time, as people became more sophisticated, blood sacrifices were omitted, but it was still a time of atonement or washing away of sins.

The early Christian theologians, centuries after the fact, gave this primitive belief new life in the concept of the "vicarious atonement." It is a hideous doctrine in the religion about Jesus that has nothing at all to do with the religion of Jesus. According to this strange tenet, God sought to save the world by sacrificing his own son on the altar as a sacrificial lamb—thus vicariously freeing all persons from sin—if they accept Jesus and his blood offering.

This has been one of the major misrepresentations by the Christian tradition. Sin has been presented as an affront to God. We have taught our children that we offend God when we sin, and that we have to appease and placate him for remission of our sins. But you can't offend God! God knows nothing of sin. "Thou art of purer eyes than to behold evil." Sin is simply the perversion in our consciousness, a frustration of our God-potential. The only absolution for sin is the realization of oneness (at-one-ment) with God. But this is not simply a worship service or a special holy day. It is an awakening of consciousness (on any day).

The practice of religion is a subtle attempt at appeasement and "reconciliation." How easy it is to go through a ritual on Sunday, and then put it all back into the "six-day closet of unconcern." The word *sabbath* (from the Hebrew *shabbath*) means *intermission*. It is not a special day, but a special discipline of consciousness on any day. It is important to have frequent "silent parentheses" or quiet times of inner prayer at intervals during the involvements of every day.

God doesn't have anything special to give you on Sunday that he doesn't give you on Friday or Tuesday. The blood pumps the same on Thursday as it does on Sunday. You have the same blood pressure, and the same surging of life through your system, the same renewal of cells every day of the week. The activity of God is always functioning because you are a spiritual being. You are a child of the universe, which is calling, relentlessly seeking, to "give you the Kingdom."

Lest I be misunderstood, may I say that I believe in the great good that can come through making a "churchgoing habit." A few important advantages of such a habit are that you make a periodically renewed commitment to the "creative intermission," and that you send your mind to school, to be stimulated by concepts designed to help you to know yourself, and to progressively release your imprisoned splendor. But there is something more: an opportunity to be part of a buildup of spiritual power to which you can give and from which you can receive . . . and, in the process, to be part of a radiance of light into the world.

The word *worship* is one of the least understood words of Western religious practice. It has normally implied a glittering spectacle in which the congregants are merely spectators, and the communion with God is done for people by professionals. Actually, the word *worship* antedates the Bible. In prebiblical times the people prostrated themselves before various idols in fear and self-abasement. The word *worship*, in the Hebrew, means to "lick at the heels like a dog." We have retained this idea in the bowing of the head in prayer, which should have no place in the prayer practice of one who has heard the universe calling.

The word *prayer*, from the ancient Sanskrit root *pal-al*, means "judging oneself to be wondrously made." The practice of prayer should lead us to lift up our eyes and know that, if we are worthy to draw a breath, we are worthy of the fullness of life. For we need a renewed sense of self-worth. This is why I have coined the word *worth-ship,* as an identification of our Sunday experiences. Thus the service is not a performance we put on for God's benefit, but a workshop in which we work for an expanded sense of self-worth. We must stop thinking of ourselves as "miserable sinners" and begin accepting ourselves as "God's own." The universe is calling us to hold our heads high and be all that we can be.

We have sung "How great thou art." But God isn't moved by our flattery. We need to know, "How great I AM," emphasizing the infinite potential that is ours to release. Of course we have to act out our greatness in love and peace in all relationships, and in keeping our mind and heart in tune with God. As Jesus said, "If you know these things, blessed are you if you do them" (John 13:17).

There is a lovely old hymn, "Take time to be holy!" This is often made to imply, "Take time to be pious!" Go to church, get down on your knees, carry a Bible under your arm. Actually, the word *holy* means whole. Oneness! Take time to become established in the awareness of "Oneness." The benefits are great: increased ability to make decisions, to unfold creative ideas, to rise above the challenges of human relations, to improve both your disposition and your health. In the marketplace of life, peace and equanimity may seem elusive, even unattainable, but they come easily to the mind that is disciplined to an experience of silence or "inner prayer." Today there is an increasing interest in prayer groups, growth groups, support groups. It is interesting to note that this is where the Christian church began. The word *church* comes from the Greek *ecclesia*, which literally means "called out ones." The early Christian movement was an activity within Judaism. It involved enlightened Jews who were into new insights of spiritual awareness. They had heard the universe calling them out of orthodoxy into an esoteric involvement with spiritual law.

In a process that tells much about human consciousness, as the generations passed the *ecclesia* became an ecclesiastical development of the churches and a uniform church liturgy. And in *ecclesiastolotry*, which means "worship of the church," a great effort was made to justify the gaudy religious edifices and the glittering spectacles of liturgical celebration within them as being a system that was specifically founded by Jesus. But a careful study of Christian history reveals that this in no way was the intention of Jesus, or of Paul, or of any of the leaders of first-century Christianity.

Thus, Christianity began as a movement within Judaism, similar to the contemporary healing movement within Protestantism. It was composed of small groups, or *ecclesia*, who met together in group prayer and in discussion of the spiritual laws revealed by Jesus. They had no buildings, and no priest or minister. It is clear that they were all faithful Jews, and not "religious renegades," for Paul clearly says that they went regularly into the temple to pray. These little bands of followers met in homes and out on the sides of hills. One of the group was chosen to be the facilitator. This is where the word *minister* began. In the beginning it had nothing whatever to do with being "ordained by God." Paul, the organizer of this growing movement, selected the leader, saying, "I ordain you." But it simply means, "I appoint you."

From this humble beginning have evolved vast ecclesiastical machines, with form and ritual and robed priests, and elaborate ceremonies, and altars and candles. We are given the strong suggestion that God is to be found in the church. Much as I noted in that small French town, multitudes of people go to church to find or experience God. But you can only experience God in yourself. God is no more present in a cathedral than in a movie theater. When you are in a sanctuary of prayer, God is present (for you) because you are present. Now, does this mean that there is a greater concentration of God in the sanctuary when a throng of people is gathered there? In other words, is there more prayer power in a prayer group than with one praying alone? Remember, the whole of God is present at every point in space. God cannot be more present anywhere than he is present everywhere.

And yet . . . there is something very special about a group, large or small. If the members of the group come with a common bond of interest, from that bonding emerges a group "soul." Jesus said, "For where two or three are gathered in my name, there am I in the midst of them" (Matt. 18:20). This is mistakenly interpreted to mean Jesus is in the midst of the group. This is one of the cases where Jesus is speaking in the absolute, referring to the transcendent awareness of the I AM. The great power of a church congregation or a small prayer group is not in the music and sermons of the service or the words exchanged in the group, but rather in a mystical process that I call "the power of the swarm." When a group, large or small, comes together in a commitment of spiritual union (or communion), that group becomes a "group soul," a consciousness to which each person gives and from which each one receives. This "soul" has its needs, and at the same time it contains the answers to its needs, which include all the needs of the people involved.

People often say to me, after a "worth-ship" service that included a lesson or lecture on truth, "How did you know my need? You were talking right to me." It is the group process at work. And in the small prayer group, when we achieve a group consciousness of unity, certain members of the group will become agents for the expression of just the right answers to another's needs.

To understand the group "power of the swarm," think for a minute of a swarm of bees, a school of fish, or a large flight of starlings. The individual entities, in some mysterious way, become locked into the whole body. A transcendent force seems to take over, controlling and guiding the whole body, creating patterns of motion so complex that they seem to have been choreographed from above. Flocks of birds and schools of fish have a distinctive style of behavior with a fluidity and a seeming intelligence that transcend the abilities of their members. The vast flight of starlings is capable of turning *en masse*, avoiding collisions within the flock—without any one leader. Fish, too, their vision limited in murky water, manage complex, seemingly instantaneous maneuvers when alarmed by an intruder.

In the prayer group or large worth-ship service, if there is a willingness to swarm, to let go of self and its ego needs, and give one's self over to the larger good of the group, there is a

145

tremendous potential for power. Required are: love, humility, and commitment to the greater good of all. If you give yourself lovingly to the group, and trust the process, you will receive a great blessing.

I am often asked, "What about Holy Communion . . . do you have communion services?" My response, "Every time we pray we have communion." "Taking communion," to many people, means "taking your place in the grandstand." There is no automatic communion for the spectator. You have to "get in the game" and "experience a firsthand and immediate experience of God." No one can do your praying for you. You can only move to your own center. Meister Eckhart shows this clear insight when he suggests you should dip into your own treasure, for you carry all reality in essence within yourself.

But having said that, there is a great power in group prayer. When people in a group can really let go their ego, and humbly let themselves merge into the group energy, there can be a buildup of that energy to a dramatic point. The prayer of the group can't heal anyone or change anyone's life. But it can become a pool of light, which may be radiated out to include specific persons or general situations in the world.

A prayer group can be effective if it meets frequently to experience a bonding. The ideal size is ten to twelve persons. If it includes more than this it becomes difficult to effect a swarming, and thus to establish the "group soul."

At the start of each session, it is helpful to take ten minutes to interact in fellowship and love. This is to renew an awareness of the bonding of the group soul. Then, most prayer groups will have a time for discussion and exchange of ideas. It is helpful if it is based on the study of an inspirational book. The text gives a frame of reference within which the sharing time will function. If the purpose of the group is the study of truth, then the larger portion of the time will be given over to the study and discussion of truth. If it is essentially a prayer group, it is still good to have some input from a book, or a brief talk by one of the group. This, too, sets a kind of boundary line within which to function.

At the beginning of the prayer portion of the session it is well to remind the group that they should not sympathetically react to problems and pain. They might decide in advance if affirmations or treatments will be voiced by the group in unison or by an individual, or if it is to be a "Quaker type" session, where they sit in silence until someone is moved to speak a word or prayer.

When the format is agreed upon, the facilitator calls for stillness, and everyone is instructed to "go down their own well" to make their own contact with the divine flow. The mistake is often made of plunging into a group prayer without taking time for each person to touch the secret spring in his or her own heart. If any participants do not make their own contact, they simply "get in the grandstand" and become spectators. And they become weak links in the circle.

After a designated period of individual communion, at the direction of the facilitator, attention is called to joining together as a group dynamo, which can, if the group wishes, be symbolized by the joining of hands around the circle. And now by the "power of the swarm" the group will function as one body.

At this point the facilitator may introduce names of persons or situations to which to direct the group prayer energy. Recall our thoughts about praying for others . . . the first step is to heal the concern. An excellent approach is to have the people visualize the people or conditions on the "prayer agenda" in the center of the circle, so that the group can symbolize the hands of the universe reaching out in support. And the voiced affirmations or treatments can be as "the universe calling" for all persons to come up higher to the greater good that it is the Father's good pleasure to give.

The important thing is to know that "it is not I but the Father . . . " As a group, project the light and power to anything that concerns you. And remember, you are not praying *to* God. You are each one opening yourself to the divine flow, and then as a group you become focused on the power of God blessing those in the center of the circle, and reaching out in a blessing of peace and love to all the world.

Now to sum up, when you attend a church service or a Sunday lecture (and you owe it to yourself to do so often), in your mind make a transposition to a service of "creative worthship." Predetermine that you will find a renewed awareness of who you really are, a whole and complete child of God. Enter the experience, not looking to find God, but confidently bringing God with you. And in the opening prayer of the service, whatever the words, you go within and "call to remembrance" your own unique oneness with the creative flow . . . so that you will not be a mere spectator in the grandstand, but an active participant, with your own resources to give.

Approach your sabbath experience in this way and you will always receive a great blessing for being there. And it will be more than a receiving, it will be a giving way to your own imprisoned splendor. And, idealistic as it sounds, the world will be a better place because you went to church that day.

CHAPTER 13

Prayer Practice for Human Needs

During the course of this book, we have presented some ideas about prayer and your relationship with God and the universe that may have been shocking, possibly even sacrilegious to you. We have stressed the idea that prayer is not about God. It is about you and your consciousness of God. Prayer is not about attempting to reach God, to communicate with him, to convince him of your worthiness, or to plead for help in your human needs. Jesus made it very clear that God knows what you need, even before you pray. More than that, God doesn't *have* what you need. God *is* what you need.

We have used the words God and universe interchangeably. That may well have been a foreign idea to you. But if God is all, can there be anything more than the all? This means the universe, the whole of things. The reason I like to use the word *universe* is that it is impersonal, free from our hangups about where God is, and what his will for us may be.

We live in an expanding universe, where growth is the nature of things. As creatures of the universe, we have a built-in, restless urge to unfold, to rise to the heights of our innate possibilities. The universe is calling. It is a ceaseless longing in the mind of the universe to outpicture in us that which we are created to become.

Prayer is not something you do to God or say to God, or a performance you put on for God. It is, in silence, finding that point in you where God is Being *being you.* You may feel that you have long since let go of the anthropomorphic idea of God. But if you are observant you may realize that you still refer to "God beside me," "God within me," "God guiding me," "God healing me." So God is still something separate from you.

You may talk about getting into the presence. But you can never get out of the presence, for the "presence" is present, all-present, omnipresent. You may say you are "practicing the presence of God." But if your thought embraces a belief in separation (God and you), you are actually practicing the "absence of God." To practice the presence is to practice oneness. Not God and me, but God, the universal creative process, expressing itself *as* me. So you can only know God as you know yourself. Without self-realization, the contemplation of God is simply dealing with an intellectual abstraction. And any prayer effort that deals only with the abstraction is an intellectual *cul-de-sac,* a dead-end street to nowhere. When Jesus says, "No man cometh unto the Father, but by me" (John 14:6, KJV), he is saying that you can't reach God in shrines or cathedrals "out there" unless you first become aware of God within. "By me" means through the I AM of your nature.

We have called this chapter "Prayer Practice for Human Needs," but it is important to realize that there is actually only one problem. Theologians call it *sin*. Paul says, "The wages of sin is death" (Romans 6:23). Sin is the consciousness of separation. And the one and only solution to the one basic problem is to reestablish a sense of oneness, to get recentered in the divine flow.

Last year we received a lovely plant for Christmas. It was a small live bush that had been filled out and shaped like a Christmas tree by inserting into the foliage many additional branches, which were, thus, not a part of the plant. The result was a strikingly beautiful tree. But as the weeks passed the supplementary branches wilted and died, for they were not connected to the plant's main trunk and rootage system. They were separated from the renewing life energy. They were "living in sin," thus they died. Can you see how futile it would have been to pray for these branches to bear fruit, or to flower?

Can you see the parallel with life's experiences? Wherever there is a challenge or need, there is somewhere in consciousness a sense of separation. And try as you may to heal the cut or bring order to the confused condition, unless you get recentered with the divine flow within, any other efforts to heal the condition will be like applying a Band-Aid. A true healing can only come through remembering who you are, a spiritual being in a spiritual universe. Thus prayer is not fixing fruit on the separated branches. It is getting in tune with the integrity of the tree and its branch and leaf system, blessing the branches that are alive, and seeing them rich with fruit. Often we are so busy trying to effect a miracle that we fail to see the natural outworking that comes if we get in tune.

If you owned a mountain cabin and wanted to make it fresh and habitable again after a long winter being shuttered up, you would not have to induce the air to enter the doors, or to plead with light to enter the unshuttered windows. The moment you open the doors and windows the wind and sunshine surge in. This is an excellent illustration of our relationship with the divine flow.

We have thought of God as one who could help if we took our troubles to him, and unburdened ourselves on his broad shoulders. But as I have said, "Don't take your troubles to God . . . God isn't into troubles." Jesus says, "Your Father knows what you need before you ask Him" (Matt. 6:8). But God doesn't know of your lack. A need is a vessel to be filled, but lack is a state of mind. God knows the need and it is his good pleasure to give you the Kingdom. But God can't change your attitude of lack.

God doesn't sit up there in his billowy cloud-heaven before a great panel of flashing lights, watching your prayer request cause a light on your name to flash on. Imagine: God says, "Oh yes, there is a call from Eric Butterworth. He's been pretty good lately. I will go down and help him." Maybe he adds, "When I can get to it." Prayer is not a way to turn on the light in God, but to turn on the light in yourself, and God is that light.

The question is asked, "If God is a presence who knows our needs even before we ask, then why are we told to ask?" This is a good question. The idea of asking God for help through prayer has become a fixation in our consciousness. I say, "Don't ask God for help at any time." If God were the anthropomorphic being we have seen him as being, can't you imagine that he would be insulted? When, despite the fact that in our creation we have been endowed with everything, we ask for more? He might say, "Such ingratitude!"

Doesn't the Bible say that we should ask God for help? If you look up the word *ask* as it is used in the Old and New Testaments, you will find that both the Hebrew and the Greek words for *ask* have a strong connotation of "claim" and "demand." When the landlord comes to the door, he might say, "I have come to ask for the rent." He is not asking for a contribution. He is demanding that which is due. When you go to the parking garage to retrieve your car, you present the claim check and you ask for your car. But you are claiming that which is yours by title. When you hold your cup under a water faucet and open the tap, you are not begging for but demanding water. The Old Testament says, "Concerning the work of my hands command ye me" (Isa. 45:11, KJV).

All the life, substance, and intelligence of spirit are yours: all that you can accept. Prayer is not begging for handouts. It is claiming your rightful inheritance. Life is consciousness. When you form the consciousness that makes the result inevitable, your answer will manifest itself.

For a healing need: Work for the realization that health is natural. Let go of the "sickness syndrome." How often have you heard, "I have gone three months without a cold. I have really been lucky"? Modern medical research is rapidly approaching the view that sickness doesn't belong in the human experience. We have been told, "God created man upright, but he has sought out many inventions." Sickness is an invention of human consciousness. Health is natural. The illness is simply a concealment of the allness. But there is always in you that which is whole, an allness that is present even within your illness.

Your prayer for healing should not be an attempt to fight sickness, but to know and release your wholeness. Remember, in divine mind there is a perfect counterpart to any disease or weakened cell or organ of the body. This is the basis of spiritual healing. Within you is the unborn possibility of limitless life, and yours is the privilege of giving birth to it.

Paul says, "Awake thou that sleepest . . . and Christ shall give thee light" (Eph. 5:14, KJV). Haven't you fantasized about waking up one morning to find that all the trials and difficulties of your life have disappeared? That it was all just a bad dream? That fantasy originates in the universe calling you to "come up higher." Your prayer is not to convince God to give you something that you don't have, rather it is to awaken to the realization of your wholeness in God-mind, the perfect spiritual counterpart to the human limitation. The answer to your prayer, thus, is not something that is given to you from other sources, by divine fiat or even by mental manipulation. It is an answer that was present in the universe even before you began to pray. And as a matter of fact, even if you do not know it, your decision to turn to prayer was an intuitive response to the universe calling you, which came first. Thus, if we really understood the healing process, we would realize that the universe seeks to enfold you in healing life to a degree even greater than you desire it for yourself. Gibran reflects this amazing insight when he says that it is God's will in us that wills and his desire in us that desires.

For a prosperity need: First, we need to get out of the pie-in-the-sky concept of prayer that suggests a Brink's truck rolling up to your door bringing bags of currency and coins. There is no magic and certainly no miracle involved in the demonstration of abundance in our lives. Prayer deals in consciousness. When you have a lack consciousness, you inhibit the natural flow of the universe in your life. This consciousness frustrates jobs and salaries and general income, as a beaver's dam effectively blocks the flow of a stream. And when you have a prosperity consciousness, you are consciously in the flow of the abundance of the universe that rushes and streams and pours into you from all sides.

There is no lack in the universe. Lack is simply a state of mind that separates us from the divine flow. Don't let lack become a part of your prayer. Know the truth of omnipresent supply. Don't pray for lack, unemployment, or failure, for this serves to emphasize them and treats them as if they were real. Let your prayer be to establish you in the awareness that you

157

live and move and have your being in a sea of infinite substance, as a fish lives in water.

There is a divine mind counterpart for every human need.
There is an answer for every problem, substance for every financial requirement, and a job for every willing worker. The eco-
nomic indicators may not tell you this. You need to tell it to
yourself, for economics is a spiritual process. As far as your
experience in the marketplace is concerned, you make the
difference.

Take time, occasionally, to visualize yourself settling com-
fortably in the universal flow of substance cascading into you
and through you. Then you might want to speak the word of
truth: "I am prospered and successful." Not to make it true,
but to identify with that which is true.

Making decisions: Get the realization that there is an answer
in God-mind even before you ask . . . and you are a state of
consciousness in God-mind. Don't try to make a decision, ever.
Your need is to *discover* a decision. So let go the pressures of
standing at a crossroads, fearing that a wrong choice will be a
disaster. Emerson had the conviction that there is guidance for
us at all times . . . and by "lowly listening" we will always hear
the right word.

The frustration of decisions is the fear of making the wrong
ones. It is important to know that you can't make a wrong
decision. The choice you make will lead you into the experience you need, to earn the right to the higher consciousness

in which a more productive choice will be made . . . for life is growth.

You may want to affirm: "I know what to do, and I do it." And as you speak those words, you tune into a conscious flow, which is the condition that makes the result inevitable. If you are facing a crossroads decision, write out some of the pros and cons of the project. Ask yourself some pertinent questions such as "What do I really want?" and "Why?" Then lay it all aside, give it an incubation period. Finally, at a predetermined "aliveline" ("deadline" is too negative) have your prayer. Relax and get a sense of complete release. Go inward to feel your oneness with the guiding intelligence of the universe. Affirm, "I know what to do and I do it." Then do it! And it will be right.

In every need for direction or decision, the universe is calling. Prayer is a kind of listening . . . not expecting to hear a voice, but to feel a presence . . . a guidance. It is common to think of prayer as constant treatment or spoken words of affirmation. But the words are a conditioning of our own consciousness that are of little help unless we listen. Otherwise it is like a student coming to a classroom, telling the teacher some things, leaving before the instruction begins, then saying, "They don't teach you anything in this school."

Your diligent practice of the science of prayer should give you a deep feeling of respect for the guidance principle, and lead you to "trust the process."

Prayer for a business or any activity in which you are interested: Every business or activity of people has a certain mental atmosphere of its own. This energy pattern decides what will be drawn to it. And this is what we have to work with. Let go of your preconceptions and prejudices, your memory of injustices and unjust people, and of course your own anxious concern about it all.

It takes only one person to open a window or turn on the air-conditioning unit. And it takes only one person to start the prayer-conditioning process. Relax . . . let go . . . move into the "still point." Reflect on the flow of the universal harmony. Then affirm: "Divine order and harmony are now established in this business (office, school, church, political assembly)."

Remember, we are dealing with a creative process that needs only a channel, not a ritual or a well-formulated spiritual treatment. Care must be used to keep from thinking that the treatment or the words are making things happen. The point is, the divine process is already in you. You don't have to do anything or reach for anything. You don't have to contact God and beg for a miracle. You need only to know, really know, that the universe is calling. Listen, accept, and BE.

Admittedly, prayer may seem at times to work wonders. But the wonder-working potential is always within you, waiting to be released. You may think that I oversimplify by outlining the prayer technique as I have. And I admit that I am making it appear simple . . . because it *is* eminently simple. Of course, let me add, *it is not easy.* It takes much practice and discipline. But the reward is great . . . Jesus called it "the life more abundant."

The Formula

In readying your mind for a prayer experience, always remember that there is a divine mind counterpart for every human need. In other words, whatever you are seeking to pray about, there is an answer that is at once a pattern and a plan for its unfoldment. You do not make this answer. It exists within the depths of your super-conscious mind, even before you have the awareness of a need. And the very fact that you are approaching the situation in prayer means that you have intuitively sensed that the universe is calling.

Take a few moments to reflect on just what it is that you are praying about. Be clear on this. Can you imagine an airline pilot taking off and, when he has reached the cruising altitude and the plane is leveled, letting go of the controls and saying, "I wonder where the plane is going to take us today?" Think about that!

Have a period of relaxation. If necessary, go through a drill in relaxing the various parts of the body. Visualize your body falling into a heap on the floor like a limp dishrag. Hold your arms out and form two tight fists, and imagine that all you are concerned about is within those two fists. Then unclasp the fists, and let your arms drop into your lap, and all the concerns fall off to the floor beneath.

Concentrate your attention on a point of light deep within your mind. This is "the still point," the point where the allness of God becomes the eachness of you. Let yourself float gently down into this deep well of the mind, and as you come closer to that point of light, it becomes larger and larger, as if you were coming close to the fiery orb of the sun. Eventually you go right into and through the light, and now you do not see light, you are enlightened, and you see *from* light. Rest quietly in this awareness. This is the "ground of being" on which your prayer builds. Feel the infusion of energy and life and light. Remain in this awareness for five or ten minutes.

Now, for the first time call to mind that for which you want to pray. It may be a person, a condition, some financial need, or perhaps healing for yourself. Remember: you are in the light, and your prayer is the projection of this light, whether by words of truth (affirmation or treatment), or simply as a way to focus your light on the issue. Above all, remember that you do not pray *to* God, you pray for whatever you want *from* the consciousness of God. Don't be tense or anxious. Quietly, lovingly, with no sense of urgency, speak your word of truth, or just see the projection of light.

Feel grateful . . . and then "Amen." So be it! It is done! It is finished! How often should you pray for this matter? As often as you find yourself slipping in consciousness into fear or worry. Praying too often indicates that you are being motivated by worry. The ideal is to let go so completely that you forget you had a problem . . . or, if it comes to mind, you just visualize a focus of light going forth to illumine and bless.

This is the process. Don't make a ritual out of it. Adapt it in any way you desire to make it suitable for your consciousness. Just remember, you are not praying *to* God . . . you are praying *from* the consciousness of God.

PART THREE

BEYOND PRAYER

CHAPTER 14

After Prayer, What?

Let us suppose that you have prayed about some need, using the science of prayer. You have let go of the problem in a time of relaxation of mind and body. You have turned within in an experience of wordless silence, feeling your oneness at the center. And then you have spoken the word of truth, affirming the reality in back of the negative appearance . . . and you have ended with a consciousness of "Amen!—So be it!"

Now what do you do? At times you may come to the end of your prayer time feeling empty, doubtful, wondering if the prayer will work. Remember, God can do no more for you than he can do through you.

You may be thinking, "Well, I have prayed, so now the rest is up to God." But as they say in tennis, "the ball is in your court." Your prayer is not for God. He needs neither your prayers nor your praise. He doesn't need your supplication to understand your need. "The Father knows what things you have need of, even before you ask him." And it is always "the Father's good pleasure to give you the Kingdom." In God there is an eternal *yes*, but your part is to get into a *Yes* consciousness, and stay there. "Change your mind and keep it changed."

Your prayer time may have renewed your faith and sharpened your vision, but it is still "thy faith hath made thee whole." It is not that God has done something special for you, for God has already done all that he can ever do. He has created you in his image, and endowed you with the possibilities of the Kingdom of God within you. So God has already done his work. Your need is to believe it, and to act as if you believe it.

Jesus said, "If you know these things, blessed are you if you do them" (John 13:17, ASV). Beyond the *Amen* of prayer, the next step is to act as if you believe that what you have affirmed is really true. Go and do what comes naturally, and it will come naturally, because it is the activity of God in you that has revealed the goal, and has given you the faith in it. The Quakers have a delightful phrase, "When you pray, move your feet." Expect the answer through you . . . in guidance . . . and direction . . . through your consciousness. Get busy *being* what you have affirmed.

Often, the hoped-for demonstration is an end, a goal, a condition, or an object or achievement all wrapped up and beribboned—something about which we can sit back and say with Jack Horner, "I stuck in my thumb and pulled out a plum, and said, what a good boy am I!" In other words, I prayed . . . and the answer came . . . and it is all over.

But life doesn't come to ends. Life is an experience of growth and going on. Many persons sit in the serene attitude of "I fold my hands and wait," expecting the spirit to move them, or God's miracle to unfold.

You may say, "I am praying for a job. When God tells me where to apply I'll go there, but in the meantime, I'll watch the soaps on TV. But I am a great believer in prayer, and I am praying diligently about it." When you pray, move your feet! People often complain that they have not received their demonstration in a certain situation. Actually, they are probably holding back the process because they are not letting the demonstration make them. The ball is really in their court, but they act as if it were in God's.

The Bible does say, "Those that wait on the Lord shall inherit the earth" (Ps. 37:9). But this is another one of those cases where a dubious translation has led to confusion. To wait on the Lord doesn't mean sitting on your hands, a kind of procrastination. The Hebrew word from which we get the word *wait* is *qavah*, which literally means "to bind together." Thus, to wait on the Lord means to integrate yourself with the power and potential of your spiritual nature, to get yourself plugged in, tuned in, and turned on.

The waiting is not a matter of time, but of consciousness. We have the cliché, "in God's good time." So then, if we wait a long time and nothing happens, we have erroneously thought, "I guess God is saying 'No!' . . . or 'Not yet, dear . . .'" What we need is to get our mind to stay on God, to get and keep plugged in, to become a channel for the creative flow.

Prayer is often limited by the complex of "these things take time." However, it is not the conditions that are limited by time, but your attitude toward them. The problem will continue as long as you *hope* it will be healed "one of these days." And it will always remain one of these days . . . until you change your thought and realize that "now is the time." This is the moment. I accept it. "Yes!"

Jacob Boehme says that man fell asleep in time and can never understand himself or life until he wakes up. Paul believed this too, for he says, "Awake thou that sleepest that Christ shall shine upon you." Wake up! Accept this dynamic, radiant, child-of-God-self which is you, and has been you from the very beginning of time. When we are asleep to our true power, the reality within, we go about our life walking, talking, maneuvering in a state of unconsciousness. Our acts are the mechanical acts of hypnotized people. This is why the world seems to go from one disaster to another.

George Gurdjieff says that a conscious human being would not destroy himself through crime and war. It is just that we simply do not know what we are doing to ourselves. But he says optimistically that you can wake up. You can know who you really are, and then love, intelligence, and peace will no longer be merely words and theories. They will be you.

You see, when you close your eyes, you are opening the inner eye of transcendence, that you may see from the highest point of view. The challenge is to keep this inner eye open beyond prayer . . . and that takes discipline. The need is not to set things right, but to see them rightly.

This takes all the effort and strain out of prayer. You may say, "I have tried and tried to make this thing work and now I am going to pray for a divine outworking." But you are still *trying* to work it out, only now you are trying, through prayer, to set it right. There is a letting go called for, knowing that the need is not to set it right, but to see it rightly. And the one way is to turn from the appearance, close your eyes to all the convincing facts of the condition, and open the inner eye, the process that Jesus calls "judging righteous judgment." This means seeing it as it was intended to be.

It is like using the imaging power of the mind and seeing a sick child as a perfect, whole, radiant child, running about, bouncing a ball, riding a tricycle out of doors. Or seeing yourself as the strong, capable, competent person that you are, that you can become. "As the within, so the without." No matter what the appearance, the inner is always there. Thus prayer is to close the outer eyes and open the inner eye of transcendence, to see from the highest point of view.

You may say, "But the condition is there. My side hurts." Or, "I don't have enough money in the bank. It's a fact!" Of course it is a fact . . . but it is not the truth. Facts and truth are two entirely different things. The truth is what a thing *can* be—the reality that is always present because God is always present. He is present as that which you need, and as that which divine life is seeking to give you.

We live in a universe of law. The most effective prayer still does not bypass the obligation to live within the divine law. It takes hours of disciplined practice to become a good musician or, as I can attest, a good golfer. How many hours a day does it require to become a good truth student? I mean thinking and living spiritual principles. Just reading truth books will not make you a metaphysician, any more than reading about the violin will make you a good violinist. Something much more is required of us.

How much time should you spend in the practice of the presence of God? All the time! Because we are dealing with fundamental law—we are not dealing with the caprice of God, who may smile on you once in a while, while you must go begging, hat in hand, hoping to get into the rhythm of the creative flow once in a while. That certainly is not what prayer is all about.

How often do you have to practice the presence of gravity? All the time! Any time you forget about gravity, and fail to practice your relationship with it, you fall on your face. So with the practice of the presence of God. We are told to "pray without ceasing." It could be said that the reason we have problems is that we stop practicing the presence of God. So you see, the practice of the presence of God is not just a nice thing you do for which you get brownie points. It is something you do for survival. The sooner you realize this, the sooner you will begin to experience that life more abundant that Jesus promised.

When you open your eyes from your prayer time, potentially you are born into the world in a new level of consciousness; you are born again as a new person. Isn't that wonderful? You open your eyes and "Wow!" it is your birthday. It's a new day. You are a new person. And it can be true if you believe that life is a constant process of awakening, letting go, releasing that which is negative, getting in tune with the positive flow of divine life.

The challenge is to act as if you are new, trust the process, and let it lead you forward to a new experience, as it surely will. Your *Amen* says "OK," so it is. Believe that it is done. Again, the ball is in your court. You have prayed for the job or a relationship or for a healing. So now, move your feet. Get started. There will be the temptation of many influences urging you to postpone action, to wait until the spirit moves you, to do it tomorrow. Goethe says that whatever you dream you can do, begin it, for boldness has genius and power and magic in it.

So keep on, and keep on keeping on, until the work is completed. Your mind may be harassed by many subconscious influences, urging you to let down, drop out, give up. The fact is that those who succeed, who do great things in music and art and science and business and research and athletics, may well be different from most of us mainly because of the courage to launch themselves and the will to keep on till the goal is reached.

It is interesting how many people feel that if a thing is right, it should literally work itself out. So . . . if there are obstacles, pressures, or delays, then it must not be right for you. They think it is God's way of saying *no!*, thus it can't or shouldn't be done.

Long-distance runners are often defeated by the intrusion of negative thoughts, telling them that they can't go on. They may have the wildest illusions that they are exhausted, that they are dying, that it is impossible to continue. And if they give in, they drop out. But if they forge on through this barrier (the runner calls it *the wall*), they get their "second wind." William James had this in mind when he said that we must move past the first layer of fatigue.

Now, as we keep on and keep on keeping on in the trusting process, it is important to realize that the universe has many hands, many means by which your answer will come. A woman was looking back to her childhood where she learned a great lesson in prayer. Little girls in her day were supposed to learn to knit and sew, so every evening she had to make one piece for a patchwork quilt. Her hands were awkward, and her stubby fingers were unsuited for needlework. After an evening's work using all her ability, she had invariably produced a piece that was uneven and puckered. It was always discouraging, after trying so hard. Her mother taught her to place the pieces between the pages of the Bible on her bedstand, so that during the night God would make the "crooked places straight." And in the morning she would go to her Bible and discover that the piece was sewn tight and neat. It helped her to have a great trust in God. She said it wasn't until many years later that she learned that her mother would always tiptoe into her room while she was sleeping, pick out the stitches, and re-sew them straight. But, she says, it didn't shake her faith in God. It taught her another great lesson: that God invariably works through human hands to bring about good.

Again, trust the process . . . and keep open. A realization that has always been helpful to me is, "I have faith in God as the source of all my good, and I bless all the many channels through which it may come."

After prayer, the next step is the need to give. This may well be the problem. When things get tight, something's got to give. It is an excellent practice. At the conclusion of any and every prayer, make a commitment to give in some way. It is not that God demands it, but that it is one way to be certain that you are giving way to the flow. Don't delude yourself. Giving is an important prerequisite to receiving. Make a commitment to some effort of giving. It is a marvelous practice.

So . . . after prayer, what do you do? You discipline yourself to maintain the transcendent perspective, and keep yourself in a state of perpetual trust in the spiritual process.

There has been a lot of talk recently about Victor Hugo's *Les Misérables,* because of the hit musical of the same name. In the book, the nuns of the Convent of Perpetual Adoration are reminded of the Holy Life every half hour by the ringing of a bell. No matter what they are doing, every nun stops and repeats a Hail Mary. You can imagine that a nun on the verge of losing her temper might, by the ringing of a bell, be reminded to keep her inward peace, to maintain her prayer consciousness.

One of my favorite characters in the Bible is Nehemiah, who undertook the task of rebuilding the walls of the city of Jerusalem—a symbol of prayer. The surrounding tribes did everything they could do to harass Nehemiah in his work and prevent the wall from being completed. They conspired to have him come out to the plains of Ono for a meeting, where they would slay him. I see him standing tall upon the wall and proclaiming dramatically, "I am doing a great work and I cannot come down." It is a fine credo for the sincere student of truth.

Get the feeling that every difficulty that seems to disrupt the consciousness achieved by your prayer is like a bell ringing to remind you to reaffirm who and what you are, to remember the truth that "If you want to you can, because you couldn't want to if you couldn't. Your desire is proof positive of your ability." Realize this . . . and keep on. Your power to see a goal at all is also the power to see it through to achievement. Believe this, and act as if you believed it.

Stand tall upon the wall of your spiritual defenses, and proclaim to the harassing negative thoughts that would lure you into chaos: "I am doing a good work and I will not come down."

A man once asked Socrates, "How do I get to Mount Olympus?" The wise man said, "Just make every step you take go in that direction." This is similar to the man who stopped the great Paderewsky on the streets of Manhattan and asked, "How do I get to Carnegie Hall?" The reply? "Practice, practice, practice."

To bring this study of prayer to a close, let me challenge you to make a new beginning in the practice of prayer. For a period of study and practice, drill yourself on the most shocking aspects of this book, and follow its technique in praying about people and conditions, and about yourself. But then, when you feel you have caught the idea, you should be on a higher vibrational level, and the process should work for you as readily as you breathe. If you find things not responding to your prayers, then it would be good to go back to the technique and take another period of practice. If you really work at it, I am convinced that the process will work wonders in your life.

Remember, prayer is an inward-out activity of mind. It is not putting needs and troubles into God's mind. Rather, it is letting God-mind speak the words through you. The universe is calling . . . are you listening?

Notes

Chapter 1: A Short History of Prayer

1. Alexander Pope. "An Essay on Man." In *Familiar Quotations* by John Bartlett, p. 408. Boston: Little, Brown & Co., 1968.
2. Henry Wadsworth Longfellow. "The Song of Hiawatha." In *The Complete Poetical Works of Longfellow*, p. 114. Boston: Houghton Mifflin, 1920.
3. Eric Butterworth, *Discover the Power Within You* (San Francisco: Harper & Row, 1989), p. 34.
4. William Wordsworth. "Tintern Abbey." In *Masterpieces of Religious Verse*, p. 65. New York: Harper & Row.

Chapter 2: The Miracle Trap

1. Marc Connelly, *The Green Pastures* (New York: Ferrar & Rhinehart, 1930), p. 18, part one, scene two.
2. Henry David Thoreau, *Walden* (New York: Signet Books), p. 215.

Chapter 5: The Cosmic Counterpart

1. Ralph Waldo Emerson, *The Complete Writings of Ralph Waldo Emerson* (New York: William H. Wise & Co., 1929), p. 167.
2. Charles Fillmore, *Jesus Christ Heals* (Lee's Summit, MO: Unity School of Christianity, 1939), p. 30.
3. Emerson, *The Complete Writings*, p. 148.
4. Plotinus, from *Letters of a Scattered Brotherhood* (New York: Harper & Row, 1948), p. 103.
5. Arthur M. Abell, *Talks with Great Composers* (Garmisch-Partenkirchen: G. E. Schroeder, 1964), p. 21.

Chapter 6: *Relax, Let Go, Let God*

1. Alfred Tennyson. "The Higher Pantheism." In *Masterpieces of Religious Verse*, p. 654, stanza 6. New York: Harper & Row.
2. Emmet Fox, *Power Through Constructive Thinking* (New York: Harper & Bros., 1940), p. 36.
3. H. Emilie Cady, *Lessons in Truth* (Lee's Summit, MO: Unity School of Christianity, 1962), chapter 4.
4. Meister Eckhart, *The Perennial Philosophy* (New York: Harper & Bros., 1945), p. 175.

Chapter 7: *The Way of the Silence*

1. Quote from *The Bhagavad-Gita, a Translation and Commentary*, by Maharishi Mahesh Yogi (Oslo, Norway: International SRM Publications, 1967), p. 326.

Chapter 9: *The Great Amen*

1. William Shakespeare, *Macbeth* (New York: E. F. Dutton & Co., 1963), p. 317, act 2, scene 2.

Chapter 11: *A Word about Jesus*

1. Charles Fillmore, *Talks on Truth* (Lee's Summit, MO: Unity School of Christianity, 1962), p. 169.
2. Oliver L. Reiser, *Cosmic Humanism* (Cambridge, MA: Schenkman Publishing, 1966), pp. 406, 407.